# COUPLES COMMUNICATION

HOW TO SAVE AND CURE YOUR RELATIONSHIP
THROUGH COUPLES THERAPY, LEARNING TO
IMPROVE YOUR SKILLS AND ELIMINATING
CONFLICTS WITH A STEP BY STEP GUIDE.

**A.P. COLLINS**

contained within this document, including, but not limited to, errors, omissions, or inaccuracies.

## Introduction

In our fast-paced and modern world, where in-person communication has been replaced by online methods like social media, the success of relationships and institutions like marriage that depend highly on face-to-face conversations have suffered greatly. But it isn't all bad, as text messages and calls of any kind are still forms of communication. The problem is that people have taken to the internet and social media in such a way that they no longer seem to have the time to pay any attention to the person in front of them.

Trust, love, and commitment are a few of the things that have little chance of being fostered without communication. Talking to each other is how we developed as a species and as a society. It is what solidifies relationships. Sacrificing this for any reason at all, especially because one is too busy or for the entertainment of social media, is not a sign of positive evolution. Instead, it spells out the downward spiral that is now evident in our modern society. This 21st century is characterized by isolated individuals, procrastination, short attention spans, and comparison.

Inevitably, bad communication and its various consequences have filtered into relationships. Many couples today are especially bad at spending time speaking to each other. This is not always because both parties are not interested in making the relationship work. Many times, the problem is ignorance about the advantages of communication and how vital it is to any relationship. Today's romantic couples quite often do not have adequate knowledge on how to go about communicating with each other effectively.

The purpose of this book is to discuss the importance of communication for the benefit of couples. But even those who are not in a relationship presently can still learn something helpful from reading this book, *Couples Communication*.

## Chapter 1: How We Communicate

Communication itself has evolved over time to mean more than just the exchange of information between different parties. As a result, communication has been broken down into different forms. This chapter will capture and explain the differences in how communication is done.

When linked to a couple's relationship, the different forms of communication are looked at on grounds of how they influence the relationship. Let's consider these forms below and their varying impact on relationships.

## Verbal Communication — What is it and How Much Does It Affect Communication?

As the name suggests, verbal communication has to do with the use of speech and not the use of text. In essence, the basis of verbal communication lies in the oral factor not related to written communication.

Delving deeper, verbal communication as a term can be broken down into two separate words with traceable Latin origins. Verbal stems from the Latin root word, verbum, and communication from the word, communicare. A literal translation shows verbum to mean word, and communicare to mean share. Thus, verbal communication refers to the act of sharing by using words. Consider the evolution of communication, and verbal communication would mean the process of passing a message with words. To show the distinction in verbal communication differing from written communication, we can say verbal communication involves any method of using language and sounds as a means of passing across a message. Verbal communication serves as a tool with which concepts, ideas, desires, emotions, memories, thoughts, information, support, etc. can be expressed. It forms an important part of a relationship which is needed by both parties involved to coexist peacefully.

### Forms of Verbal Communication

There are four forms of verbal communication, namely public communication, interpersonal relations, intrapersonal relations, and small group communication. Public communication entails communication between one person or more to a group of people. interpersonal relations involve two-way communication between two people. Intrapersonal, on the other hand, involves the communication we have with ourselves. Small group communication is similar to public communication. The major difference is that the number of individuals involved is small enough for each participant to converse with another. For the purpose of couple's communication, we will consider interpersonal relations alone since a couple typically consists of two people.

### How Does Verbal Communication Affect Communication in a Relationship?

Considering the fact that verbal communication is one of the major forms of expression, it is quite significant to mention that its influence on communication in a relationship is quite vast. Couples without speech impairment employ verbal communication in literally all aspects of their relationship, ranging from dispute management, to conveying emotions, to showing support, to confiding in one another, among other things. This high importance comes with the fact that verbal communication can greatly affect a relationship in two ways; good and bad, depending on how it is employed.

In the case of oral communication, there is more to conveying a message than words. There are also the factors of tone, facial expression, and body language, which serve as the secondary features of verbal communication, forming additional meanings to the words said. Thus, it goes to show that the influence of verbal communication on relationships goes beyond the words that are being said by the parties. These other factors of speech convey an underlying meaning. This explains why a particular scenario can play out differently in a relationship depending on how it is approached. As an example, let us consider a case of dispute management. If a couple has a dispute, whether the couple uses raised voices or lowered voices will produce different results. In the case of raised voices, both parties may lose their temper and the dispute would have a higher chance of continuing than being resolved. If, however, one or both parties lower their voices and speak calmly, there is a much higher chance that they would give way to reason and the dispute would quickly be resolved.

This example just serves to show how effective tone can be in verbal communication. The sheer effect of your pitch and volume in what you say has a subconscious effect on your partner which doesn't go unnoticed. So, it is important that when speaking to your partner, whatever the case may be, you always employ the right tone. When conveying positive emotions, ensure to use a tone which shows that you mean your words. In times of negative emotions, ensure to keep a clear head and avoid raising your voice. This doesn't mean that you should suppress your emotions, but for peace to be restored, clarity is needed — and that can't be obtained from raising your voice.

Sometimes, the barriers couples face in their relationship stem from differences in translation and understanding. Simply put, the receiver understands a different meaning of what was implied by the speaker. This is a case of miscommunication as discussed in the previous book. Miscommunication factors from the influence of verbal communication in passing a message; where meaning is lost or translated incorrectly by either the speaker or listener. There are numerous reasons for this influence. On the part of the speaker, the tone, body language or facial expressions might convey very different meanings from the actual speech. Conversely, on the part of the listener, meanings may be wrongly assumed as a result of the three factors of oral communication.

In all, verbal communication serves as an integral part of any relationship because it helps both parties convey messages clearly to each other. This way, both parties are able to understand each other properly. And although there are barriers to the use of verbal communication, they don't undermine the fact that verbal communication helps tackle crisis in a relationship. If a couple shares a functional way of communication, their relationship would grow more seamlessly and there would be no case of repressed emotions — a factor which hinders communication and breaks up relationships. Take note that while it is important for you to always speak up when necessary, do not be harsh in your utterances. Communicate calmly and be transparent about your feelings to your partner.

## *Why is Verbal Communication Important?*

The importance of verbal communication in relationships cannot be overstated. There are many reasons why it is necessary for the growth and maintenance of any relationship. Below are some of the importance of verbal communication.

- Growing the relationship: For your relationship to grow, you and your partner have to make a conscious effort to communicate with each other verbally. Only then can you both reach a compromise when you have differing views. Also, verbal communication is important in finding common ground with your partner — which is a fundamental part of every healthy relationship.

- Seeking help: It's not realistic to expect your partner to be perceptive of your every need. This is sometimes a chronic case of over-expectation in relationships. It is because of this that verbal communication is important because it helps to convey intent to your partner. Communicating your problems to your partner verbally is one step in the direction of getting help. And as the popular saying goes, "A problem shared is half solved."

- Keeping your partner informed: You can't expect your partner to know all the goings-on in your life by keeping your mouth shut. This is why verbal communication is important because you can put it to use by keeping your partner up to date with what's going on in your life.

- Communicating emotions: Although it is advised that emotions are better expressed than said, it doesn't in any way undermine the fact that verbally reassuring your partner of their place in your life and your feelings towards them can be rewarding.

- Self-expression: Sometimes, the best way to express yourself to your partner is verbally. For example, in times of crisis, it is necessary that you both communicate verbally to reach an agreement and settle whatever rift there is between you both.

### *Ways of Using Verbal Communication in a Relationship*

There are tons of ways in which you can employ verbal communication to spice up your relationship. Below are a few suggestions:

- Calls: Calling your partner regularly can be a great way to maintain your relationship. If done properly, it would foster the relationship and lead to transparency and effective communication.

- Voicemails or voice notes: Sometimes, you can leave little recordings for your partner to listen to. Send them voicemails or voice notes. It doesn't have to be long and serious. It can be as simple and short as a 'hi'. Just let them know they matter to you, and that they're always on your mind even when you aren't with them.

- Talking face to face: This is the most widely used method of verbal communication. Make it a habit to always communicate with your partner face-to-face. A lot of the time, being present works better in verbal communication than other methods.

**Nonverbal Communication — What is it and How Much Does It Affect**

## Communication?

Over time, communication has evolved past the use of words alone. Although, it was possible to communicate without utterances, non-verbally, in the past, this form of communication is even more efficient now. According to research carried out by Albert Mehrabian, a psychology professor at the University of California, it was discovered that communication was only 7% verbal. The other 93% is made up of nonverbal components which make communication effective. Nonverbal communication can also be interpreted as body language, which is transmitted through the use of eye contact, tone of voice, facial expressions, and body language.

The saying, "Actions speak louder than words" cannot be any truer. When interacting with other people, the nonverbal cues you exhibit serve to convey a strong message to your audience. The way you carry yourself, move your arms, sit, walk, stand, and move your eyes all serve to give off nonverbal cues. In your relationship with your partner, the ability to use and understand nonverbal cues during communication and bonding is an effective tool for self-expression, fostering connection, and building a stronger relationship. However, the way or manner in which nonverbal cues are expressed determines the outcome of the process. If employed right, you could successfully build up a connection and a sense of trust with your partner. Otherwise, you could wind up ruining the relationship.

*Forms of Nonverbal Communication and Their Effects on Communication in Relationships*

Nonverbal communication is effective in helping people express themselves through the use of body language. The way you behave while communicating is perceived and interpreted by your audience. Thus, they are able to find meaning in both your actions and words in such a way that the former defines the latter.

Nonverbal communication takes on various forms in communication, some of which will be discussed below:

- Facial Expressions: Your face is an expressive medium through which you can communicate your emotions. More than anything, facial expressions convey your truest feelings, because they cannot be easily feigned. Even when they are, disparities still exist that expose the difference between your true emotions and the fake ones. Take note of this when communicating with your partner and stay true to whatever emotions you feel. Sometimes, one of the inhibitions to communication in relationships arise from repressed emotions evident on the face. Usually, one party ends up doubting the transparency of the other, and couple's crisis can set in. You don't want to be the partner who says everything is fine while wearing a long face. Emotions that are commonly expressed through facial expressions include happiness, surprise, fear, sadness, and anger.

- Gestures: Gestures are such an integral part of our lives that we don't even know we perform them sometimes. They are so innate we are incapable of having conversations without making some sort of gesture. Typically, gestures come in the form of arm or hand movements through which a speaker gives more meaning to his or her words. Gestures have become an inherent part of our lives so much that communicating without it could be seen as a sign of deception. In all your dealings with your partner, be careful not to transmit the wrong meanings with your gestures. Sometimes, gestures can be wrongly interpreted due to many different reasons such as miscommunication and cultural differences. These factors can play a key role in how your partner interprets your gestures, so it is imperative that you stay mindful when expressing yourself using your hands or arms.

- Eye contact: Eye contact is an important cue in nonverbal communication. Next to facial expressions, the eyes specifically are the next nonverbal components that convey one's true feelings and thoughts. It is often said that the eyes never lie, this is very true. The reason for this is because, even when emotions are feigned, the eyes would often betray the truth. For example, when smiling, the smile typically reaches the eyes — showing that the joy is from within. However, when the smile is fake the emotions don't get to the eyes and is just shown on the face. The same applies to many other emotions as well sadness, pain, fear, among others.

There are many different eye movements which have become well-known over time and have transcended cultural barriers to imply the same meaning during communication. For example, shifty eyes are thought to be a sign of deception, and rolling your eyes is thought to be a sign of boredom or disbelief. Then, there is maintaining eye contact which serves to prove that someone is genuine and interested.

- The voice: The influence of the voice on communication cannot be overlooked. As a matter of fact, your voice matters a lot in every conversation you have because sometimes, focus is given to how you sound, not what you say. Thus, tone of voice, inflection, pitch, and speed are the important nonverbal components. When this is considered, it is easy to see why many different meanings can be interpreted within a single statement. As such, for proper meaning to be conveyed, it is important that you employ the right components of your voice to match your feelings. This is because when approaching certain matters in your relationship, the elements of your voice are key determiners in deciding the outcome of events sometimes.

### How Important is Nonverbal Communication in Relationships?

Nonverbal communication makes for an important factor in developing relationships because of the impact it has on the couple and the relationship itself. If employed right, nonverbal cues can help couples explore and understand one another better through interaction. Both partners would be able to read each other's emotions. Over time, both partners would come to respect and trust the transparency of each other, and thus, trust is built in the process.

However, in trying to grow your relationship with your partner, take note that the influence of nonverbal communication can swing both ways (negative and positive). That is, nonverbal communication can be the downfall or a stepping stone for your relationship. For this reason, it is imperative that you and your partner remain mindful of nonverbal cues when talking to avoid miscommunication when in dialog. Being sensitive to nonverbal cues will help you in your relationship to communicate better and build a better relationship with your partner.

### The Effects of Nonverbal Communication on Relationships

Below are some ways nonverbal communication can affect relationships:

- It improves understanding: In communication, nonverbal cues influence the message passed from a speaker to a receiver. It enhances the receiver's understanding of what the speaker says. For instance, if you are talking with your partner and you find them nodding along as you talk, that sheer motion of their head implies that they aren't confused or put off by your words. This simple motion of the head has indicated understanding on their part. On your part, you now know that you have had effective communication.

- It defines the relationship between couples: When a good level of nonverbal communication exists between a couple, it may influence the way they react to each other so much so that they will tend to reflect each other's body language during communication. They will typically share similarities in their arm motions and exhibit similar facial expressions like smiling together and fully facing each other. All these nonverbal cues serve to influence their relationship for the better as they build rapport over time, and bond in more ways than one.

- It improves bonding: Sometimes, what communicates the depth of emotions partners have for each other comes from more nonverbal than verbal cues.

## Paraverbal Communication — What is it and How Much Does It Affect Communication?

One aspect of communication that is seldom ever talked about is the paraverbal component. The paraverbal component of communication refers to any level of modulation in the voice during communication. That is, the way and manner in which a speaker utters their words. As an example, when speaking, you can tell if the speaker is annoyed, happy, sad, etc. The paraverbal component of communication accounts for about 30% of the way we communicate as people. Think of the paraverbal component of communication as a combination of both the nonverbal and verbal components of communication. Because in detecting the tone of a speaker, verbal communication has to occur, and in associating the modulation or level of the speaker to an emotion, nonverbal communication in terms of body language, tone of voice, facial expressions, etc. has to be evident.

Paraverbal communication simply involves all the subtle details that go into a speaker's voice to imply his or her moods or thoughts. A core aspect of paraverbal communication is the choice of words and tone of voice. When angry, people tend to speak at a rapid rate and with an increasing pitch as aggression is usually manifested by a high voice pitch. In the case of certainty, people will typically look calm and collected such that the voice exhibits clarity and confidence — a sharp contrast to uncertainty in which one would look the exact opposite. When one feels attacked, one would tend to react by making curt-sounding remarks. In addition, the paraverbal is how you are able to note that your audience is bored with your company from the slow, monotonic replies the latter would give.

Like the verbal and nonverbal components of communication, the paraverbal can also be misread due to disparities that exist across cultures. Since different cultures have accents peculiar to them and the paraverbal component hinges more on the voice and choice of words, the chances of miscommunication are quite high when reading paraverbal expressions. People will often tend to end their utterances in upward or downward notes which are independent of their moods, if in this instance their ending notes are used to assume their moods, chances of incorrect assumptions are high. However, in communication, the paraverbal component trumps the verbal component because it isn't easily faked as opposed to the latter. For instance, when your partner assures you that they are not angry (verbal communication) but says so at a higher pitch and a fast rate (paraverbal communication), you can be sure their words are untrue. Some research on lies state that paraverbal expressions are a good way to look for any conscious attempt at deceit.

Seeing as paraverbal expressions form an important part of communication, how does it affect relationships? Easy. Just like nonverbal cues, when done right, paraverbal expressions give you an insight into the emotions, mood, and thoughts of your partner. It is why being mindful of your partner's paraverbal expressions is important in couples communication. It gives off the subtle details you may not necessarily notice in your partner's utterances and can help you avoid couple's crisis in most cases. Like in cases of repressed emotions and disputes, you can note the paraverbal expressions of your partner and know when it is necessary to raise the white flag. For instance, say you are talking to your partner and he or she gets put off by something you said, and rather than call it out to be addressed, they bottle it up with their emotions. If you pay no heed to the paraverbal component of their communication, you might not realize that they are actually put off, and there is no telling how far this repressed emotion can go or what it can lead to. Chances it could lead to a crisis of some sort is high if it continues to be repressed.

On the other hand, in the case of disputes, say you both can't seem to agree on a subject. If you notice the tone of your partner rising and their voice speed doubling; it might just be time to put off the discussion to avoid emotions flaring. It is important that you take into consideration your own paraverbal expressions when communicating as well as that of your partner to effect proper communication and avoid all the mishaps that come with miscommunication and ignorance.

## Components of Paraverbal Communication

There are three basic components of paraverbal communication to consider when communicating with your partner. They include:

**1. Pitch**: Pitch refers to the certain frequency or note in which the voice is sounded. In simple words, pitch is the key in which your voice is on. Over time, through research and studies, several pitches have been associated with distinct emotions and states, some of which are outlined below;

- High pitch: High pitches are often associated with the emotions of anxiety, anger and states of aggression.

- Low pitch: Low pitches are often related to states such as seriousness, authoritativeness, and emotions like sadness and fear.

The pitch of your voice is important when communicating with your partner because of the underlying message it might convey to them.

As such, it is important to note that your partner will pick up hints from the pitch of your voice, find meaning in it, and react accordingly. Another aspect of pitch to consider is variation in flow. The variation of your voice pitch is equally as important in communication as the pitch itself because it can easily be interpreted by your partner. If your voice naturally possesses a high or low pitch, it is important that your partner is aware of it so it doesn't aid miscommunication, or is misread for something else during communication. Whatever the case, ensure to pay close attention to your pitch when talking to your partner and ensure your pitch or any variations that might ensue reflects your exact meaning, emotions, and thoughts. If all these are brought in alignment with your pitch, you would have successfully avoided certain inhibitions to communication, and be able to approach the resolution of issues more objectively.

**2. Tone**: Tone of voice is one factor that is present even when pitch and speed — the other two components of communication— are discussed. This stresses its overall importance in communication. Let's find out more about tone.

Tone of voice simply refers to the manner of speaking in terms of rhythm, pitch, speed, accent, among others. Tone in itself refers to a certain pitch. Comparing both meanings, it can be deduced that tone influences the underlying meaning of communication in more ways than one. Have you ever been in a conversation with your partner and they say that they dislike your tone? If yes, do you remember taking a moment to consider how you spoke? In that instance, your partner was not implying that the words you said were foul, demeaning or patronizing. They implied that the different pitches emanating from your voice were creating a mood or exhibiting an emotion that was much disliked or uncalled for. Your partner was simply reacting to the paraverbal component of tone used in communication which gave off an underlying meaning.

Your tone of voice can influence your relationship in various ways, meaning it is important that you pay close attention to it when communicating with your partner. Below are some tips for communicating in the right tone;

- Monitor your feelings as they can easily affect your tone of voice.

- Communicate in a firm tone which conveys your implied meaning.

- Always strive to keep a low tone even in the face of problems. You stand a better chance of having effective communication when your voice isn't raised.

**3. Speed**: The rate at which you speak your words is another component of paraverbal communication worth noting. The speed of your utterances determines the quality of your communication with your partner. If you speak too fast, you might become difficult to hear and understand, which would result in your partner making assumptions. Conversely, if you speak too slowly, chances are your partner would avoid having conversations with you, as they always get bored doing so. You just have to find the right speed at which your words convey the correct meaning and can be easily understood.

Speed can also affect the emotional quality of your communication with your partner. High-speed talking will tend to make your partner feel rushed or anxious and would give off the notion that you are in a hurry, angry, or being aggressive. Conversely, a slow pace will make your message seem boring and unimportant to your partner and would give off the notion that you are not ready to communicate or are sad.

When communicating, it's best to adopt a moderate speed as it gives your partner the chance to listen, process, understand your message and keep up with you.

## Chapter 2: Without Dialogue the Couple Bursts!

When was the last time you had a conversation with your partner which didn't involve your children, work, money, problems, or other "pressing matters"? Isn't it disappointing that outside of the construct of these issues, people seldom spend a substantial amount of time talking to their partners? In this day and age, with the many different means of communication aimed at fostering connection, it is unfortunate that most relationships are two individuals who are as disconnected as they come. Most relationships seem to be lacking the genuine connection only communication can bring. And rather than speak to each other as communication ought to be, many partners speak at or past each other —it has become so normal they can't tell the difference. As a matter of fact, partners almost always never listen to each other, and this is one reason for crisis in many relationships.

Communicating in relationships now seems like a largely unpracticed concept. Communication has become a monologue, if not a characterized soliloquy, in which one party does most of the talking and the other party is either struggling to listen and understand or not listening at all. Every day of people's lives is characterized by numerous messages floating about the web from one end to another through different forms of social media. But, through all of these back and forth torrents of content, is anyone — sender or recipient — truly attentive to what is being said, or are people just caught up in mindless daze until a subject that triggers them comes up? And if they are attentive, do they understand the message being passed on? The problem with communication in present times is that it is more babbling than actual communication.

The noise is proof that people barely know how to effectively communicate. People simply haven't developed the skill of listening and hearing each other out long enough to draw meaning, indulge in meaningful interpretation of communication at all levels, or seek common ground to better interpret meaning. But it isn't like we don't possess the skill set or know-how - it's just that we don't apply it. If in any way your relationship revolves around such type of communication —where neither party is attentive and interpretation of the message is not made— then it is about time you changed the narrative. Sure, couples have to talk about issues that concern the relationship, but don't they also deserve a time out to just get to know each other better and enjoy each other's company? The key point of communicating is being able to discuss just about anything and everything with your partner. And, no, it's not subjects like tuition fees for the kids, the mortgage, or the broken faucet. Just you guys — your alone time.

Remember the time before kids and unpaid bills, when you both could chat for hours on end without knowing what discussion could lead to another? That was communicating. You were getting to know each other better. The relationship was growing. You both were growing. As a matter of fact, that could have been the healthiest stage of the relationship. But what happened? Why did communication suddenly grow cold? Why does everything now revolve around a subject very much unrelated to you both or your interests? Why does your communication now seem like a job report where you have to provide a briefing on the goings-on with the company? Why are your answers now mechanical? You don't really talk anymore. What happened?

## Let's Talk About Dialogue

Dialogue is a form of communication aimed at improving common perspective and purpose of those involved. The process of having dialogue revolves around exploring new viewpoints and ideologies, listening empathically, revealing unchecked assumptions, and seeking common ground. When done right, having dialogue can be beneficial in a relationship. It can help resolve mistrust, overcome miscommunication, and help partners reach a mutual sense of direction. In the case of conflict management, creating dialogue can help both partners reach new alignment on plans and objectives. The partners will end up gaining new insights and viewpoints, gain improved levels of creativity, and strengthen the bonds of the relationship. But dialogue isn't just about talking. It isn't just any other form of communication either. Dialogue should not be mistaken for other forms of communication because it is a class of its own in itself. It isn't a debate which involves defending a certain perspective, arguing for or against points, or inferring the meaning of others. Unlike discussion, it doesn't spring up just anywhere. Dialogue can only occur when the participants involved respect and trust one another enough to put aside bigotry and judgments, and actually listen to one another. Also, unlike negotiating, dialogue doesn't involve reaching a mutual agreement or agreeing on a plan.

### *How to Have Effective Dialogue*

It's not enough to want to dialogue alone. You and your partner must be committed to making it as effective as possible. To do this, below are some rules for having effective dialogue;

- Don't mistake having dialogue for discussion, negotiating, or debating. You can do all three of them while communicating and it still wouldn't be dialogue.

- Turn your focus on the common interests you share rather than the differences in your perspectives.

- Bring to light and clear up any assumptions which could result in miscommunication or inhibit further communication.

- Bring up general issues using concrete instances of actual happenings.

- People tend to focus on assumptions and beliefs pertaining to them before giving thought to that of others, so keep in mind that listening is a key part of dialoguing so you don't get caught up in your own thoughts.

- Don't bring in a third party to validate your point of view. Instead, agree to disagree.

- Your focus should be on addressing disparities in your value systems and not your partner.

- Set your sights on practical goals for the dialogue and try to minimize mistrust by being transparent with your choice of words.

- The aim is to foster a better relationship between you and your partner and make communication as fluid as possible.

- It is necessary that you and your partner not suppress emotions but bare them at the right time. Also, you both should not hold back on sharing personal values.

## *Practicing Dialoguing in Your Relationship*

Getting better at dialoguing comes with practice. So, here are some practice tips you can use when dialoguing with your partner.

1. When talking, try your best to keep your answers as brief, precise, and clear as possible. Taking a long time before letting your partner talk or dilly-dallying when answering a question can be off-putting for your partner; building resentment in the process rather than bonding. However, despite making your answers brief, do not hold back the truth. Just be straightforward and keep things simple.

2. Exercise calmness when dialoguing. Avoid rushing through topics like a pop quiz. Take your time to study your partner and learn about them. Paying attention to them would help draw your attention to certain components of their communication you wouldn't otherwise have noticed. Dialoguing takes time, so be prepared for it — don't try to end it all in a matter of hours. If you can't finish in one day, there is always another, so don't rush anything.

3. Always begin your dialogue with subjects that aren't sensitive. You don't want to scare off or frighten your partner with an out-of-nowhere topic and catch them off guard. The aim of dialoguing is to reconnect or begin a connection, not a means to an end to lash out at your partner. Play it cool.

4. When talking about sensitive issues, try your best to shorten the time spent on these conversations. This in no way implies that you rush through it all. Just make the discourse as simple and brief as possible and continue on with another less sensitive subject. You don't want your partner suddenly becoming defensive, and the dialogue turning into a debate or negation. Your communication would tend to become

exhausting at this point. You can schedule a specific time to talk about sensitive issues. It can be an hour, an evening, or a day of the week. Just ensure to end all discussion pertaining to sensitive issues within the allocated time frame.

5. When communicating, you and your partner should take turns speaking so that one of you is listening when the other is speaking and vice versa. If both of you speak at the same time, meaning would be lost in the process, and the communication would not be dialogue. Also, if one partner is the only one speaking while the other constantly listens, it could result in many different inhibitions plaguing the relationship. To overcome this, you and your partner should take turns asking each other's opinions on the different subjects of discussion. You can take turns in one conversation.

6. Keep in mind that one key factor in dialoguing is self-expression. The reason being that one of the goals of dialogue is to be transparent and honest about the subject of discussion. So, when speaking and listening, remember to refrain from interfering when your partner is speaking, because it can be off-putting and distracting. Also, avoid moral or personal prejudice, just focus on what your partner is saying because having a biased or judgmental mindset would only create mental blocks in your mind even without your knowledge. That way, you end up listening only to argue or debunk rather than listening to actually understand your partner's point of view. In the end, the conversation becomes a debate instead of the preplanned dialogue.

7. It is important that you are honest in your communication, but do not see it as a reason to throw caution and self-control to the wind. Just because honesty and transparency is required doesn't mean you have been given leeway to let out every other thought you have floating around in your head. Exercise self-control and carefully choose

your choice of words. Some words cannot be taken back, and their influence on your relationship may be devastating, irreparable even. Don't think that since you have to be open, you go about it without caution. This doesn't imply that you should hold back either. Modesty in your choice of words and self-control in delivery is key, and both factors are what would make your conversation a dialogue rather than a debate.

8. As much as possible, try to keep to the positive side in every conversation. Sure, the conversation will take a swing in all directions, and eventually you'll have to discuss sensitive issues that may sometimes involve painful experiences. But, in doing this, ensure to keep the discussion as brief as possible. Reminiscing on past happenings that hurt is dangerous because the longer you indulge in these memories, the more the pain will persist. You may begin to recall memories of the painful event, and before you know it, you are emotional and cannot have productive dialogue. Always remember to be as concise and precise as possible when engaging in such dialogues.

9. In dialoguing, your focus should be on finding mutually accepted perspectives in all your conversations, especially in times of conflict or crisis. In times of crisis or conflict in the relationship, you and your partner tend to have a heightened sense of the disparities that exist between you both. These differences are what cause you both to drift apart and break the connection you both may share. In dialoguing, look at changing that narrative. Turn your attention to the commonalities you both have — the things you both agree on. This is what makes an argument different from a dialogue.

10. Memories of past happenings can be reflected upon and occasionally talked about, not dredged up to take down one another. This would only destroy your rapport and result in crisis in the

relationship. Respect whatever memories you both have. So, if your partner reminisces on a memory, rather than become judgmental, try respecting and appreciating the fact that they are open enough to share it with you.

### *What Are the Reasons Why We Do Not Dialogue?*

There are many inhibitions to dialoguing. Some are external factors, others are internal, but either way, they both influence the way partners dialogue. It is necessary that you understand these reasons as they are beneficial in helping you contain any future disagreements which may arise in relation to dialogue. It would also help you affect proper dialogue. Some of the reasons why partners do not dialogue include but not limited to the following:

1. Tensions caused by the foreign environment

External to a relationship, there are certain factors which affect the way a relationship works. These factors include work, health, family, friends, among others. As much as these factors can sometimes act as the building blocks for a better relationship, they can sometimes be the bomb in a hole. Your family, friends, and work can sometimes be key determiners of how you dialogue with your partner. Since they can affect you both individually and collectively in different ways, the effect they can have on how you communicate with your partner is evident.

Let's consider your upbringing, your family and friends were integral in the process. As such, you owe a lot of the elements — personality, belief, perspective, etc. — which make up who you presently are to those factors. The same applies to your partner. So, over the years up until the moment you met your partner, you've lived and acted under the influence of both your friends and families. Together, all three factors make for the person you are now — as it does for your partner. Putting this together under the union of a relationship, you get two distinct people coming from different backgrounds and raised on different ideologies. There are bound to be disparities in their lifestyles which could inhibit dialoguing. But this is not the main cause of tension in relationships.

Up until the moment you entered the relationship, your family, friends and work decided your life. But when the script changed and you entered a relationship with someone, you didn't expect the narrative to be the same, right? Hopefully, you did not. But this is where many relationships fail. Tension manages to creep into relationships because partners do not seem to understand that a new script and a new cast implies a different narrative than before. It is simply you and your partner now. Other aspects of your life matters, but the way you communicate should not be affected by everything. It is up to you both to make decisions regarding the relationship without external influences. Don't let your family or friends play the third wheel in your relationship - it doesn't work that way.

Everything outside of your partner belongs there — outside, not in the relationship affecting things. You can't keep neglecting your duties to your partner and the relationship because of your work. Eventually, your partner is going to catch on to the fact that you don't really care, and tension festers. Over time, you both lose touch and go back to being strangers.

2. Closed character of the partner

Another factor that can inhibit dialogue in a relationship is the personalities of the partners. A key part of dialoguing involves being open and transparent with one another about what is being discussed.

But, if one or both partners remain closed off and do not open up, it is impossible for dialoguing to occur.

A closed character typically stems from many different reasons such as the fear of being judged, closed-mindedness, bias, inclusion of a third party, among others. If your partner fears being judged, they would not want to open up to you during dialoguing and will maintain a closed character in such a way that they give off little to no information at all. On the other hand, if your partner is closed-minded about certain issues, they would be on the defensive when you bring up a dialogue about them. This might lead them to adopt a closed character in which they have no desire to talk about such sensitive topics. In the case of third party intrusion; it might not sit well with your partner if you always share your discussions with third parties. It could lead them to adopt a closed character for fear of third parties knowing of sensitive information about them.

3. We use the wrong way to communicate

Imagine a public speaker addressing a stadium full of people without a microphone or speakers. Imagine the effort he or she would have to put into trying to get a message across to the audience. Imagine the strain of the effort on the speaker's person. As you ponder on this example, ponder on what the speaker is doing wrong. Communicating with the wrong medium. The exact same way the public speaker has to toil and strain to get his message across without a proper system designed for such communication, is the exact same way your relationship toils and strains when you communicate in the wrong way.

Every relationship grows with communication, but not every act of exchanging information can be called communication. There has to be a transmitter and a recipient for communication to occur. But, the availability of both transmitter and recipient is not enough. Both have to understand the message that is sent and be able to decode it. Only then can communication be said to have occurred. So, analyze your communication with your partner. Are you doing it right? Are you like the public speaker screaming at the top of your lungs without having any communication? Are you hearing but not listening? You have to learn to communicate right. Find the method that works best for you and your partner.

4. Mutual intolerance

Do you remember a kid during your school days who you just couldn't stand? That one kid who put you off with his presence no matter what time of day it was. Picture that narrative in your relationship. How do you think your dialogue would fare if you and your partner couldn't stand each other? Great? Of course not.

It's one thing for one partner to be unable to tolerate the other, but when both of them are in on the intolerance game — it's a different ball game altogether. The fact you can't tolerate each other means that you both would be unable to agree to a dialogue. And in the case that you do, the chances of an honest, open, and transparent conversation being had is significantly low. The thing with intolerance is that it builds up mental barriers in people which puts them on the defensive, especially with someone they are intolerant of. In this case, communication would be done with mental prejudice, and both partners would merely be present to hear and try to counterbalance each other.

5. Suppressed emotions

Consider suppressed emotions to be similar to a closed character. One partner simply holds on to emotional pain and covers it up. This partner does their best to not show the hurt, and anything that attempts to uncover the hurting emotion would be fought against by them. So, it would be a typical scenario for that partner to close off on sensitive issues. He or she may not want to talk or hear about issues relating to the suppressed emotions. Thus, bringing up a case of closed character.

## Chapter 3: What Are the Negative Effects of Wrong or Non-existent Communication on a Couple?

### Decline in connection

Picture yourself not talking to your partner for a long time, or talking without receiving any replies. Over time, you will discover that both of you start drifting apart. The love you both share would vanish as would the passion. And that spark that once ignited into flames every time you were with each other would die out. Eventually, your bond would be severed and you would return to being strangers — almost like you never met.

Wrong or nonexistent communication in a relationship opens the door to factors that would plague the relationship. Neither you nor your partner would see being together in the light you used to see it in previously. Of course, every relationship is bound to go through rough patches every now and then, but the occurrence of nonexistent or wrong communication cannot be overcome without conscious action. It is important that you prioritize good and effective communication in your relationship if you want to keep and grow your bond with your partner. The results can be pretty devastating when you lose touch with your partner.

**You tend to move away from the partner (we tend to keep everything to ourselves, facing problems alone and not seeing the partner as a point of reference)**

When communication in a relationship is either wrongly done or nonexistent, both partners may feel like they are in a relationship with a stranger. During times in your relationship when you and your partner don't really talk, you discover how you both begin to drift apart from each other. When you reach a point in your relationship where you and your partner are unable to understand each other on the grounds of wrong or nonexistent communication, you will notice many different signs like closed character behavior in which your partner will tend to keep to themselves. In keeping to themselves, they would prefer to face and address their problems alone without confiding in you, unable to see you as a pillar of support.

Thus, you would typically find your partner exhibiting behaviors they can't explain to you, choosing instead to crawl into their own shell and leave you in the dark wondering what went wrong. Instead of leaning on you for support, they might resort to inviting third parties into situations you might not even be aware of just to avoid striking up a conversation with you. In other cases, they might resort to behaviors like excessive drinking or drug abuse or staying out late — all for the purpose of avoiding your company. Eventually, the intrusion of third parties, the closed character behavior, and the odd behaviors would take a toll on the relationship until it bursts at the seams.

**Looking elsewhere for support**

The strength of every relationship lies in the partners' ability to support each other in times of need. As a couple in a relationship, you should be the first person your partner looks to for support, and vice versa. However, when wrong and nonexistent communication is concerned, the narrative can easily swing the other way. At first, it may not seem like a big deal when your partner starts seeking moral support outside of the relationship, but over time, you would come to see how devastating it can be.

Initially, it would begin with your partner's inability to open up to you about the happenings in their life. Next, the feeling of being able to communicate with or understand each other sets in. This is usually the final straw which breaks the ladder of support holding up the relationship. Eventually, you both become more like roommates or acquaintances than a couple. Wrong and nonexistent communication diminishes support in a relationship in the following ways:

### *Easily dismissing their perspectives*

When you are quick to silence your partner, or declare their viewpoints as unimportant, they will just as quickly begin to lose trust and respect for you. Over time, as their trust and respect diminishes, they will no longer consider you to be supportive.

### *Offering no help during decision-making processes*

The worst time to be a deadbeat partner is when big decisions are about to be made. They will lose their faith in you to provide support when making crucial choices, and they would not readily look to you for support in the future.

### Unnecessary over-criticism

Choosing to unnecessarily criticize your partner too much can be rather off-putting to them. In the end, it might drive them away to seek support elsewhere.

### Inability to motivate or inspire

If as a partner you are unable to help your partner reach greater heights through motivation and inspiration, you would undoubtedly be left out on their list of people to turn to for support.

### Arguing without arriving at a solution

If dialogue isn't taking place during communication, chances are other forms of communication like discussion, debate, or negotiation is going on. In the case of wrong or nonexistent communication, dispute management becomes a relatively difficult thing for a couple for reasons. Wrong or nonexistent communication implies that both partners are unable to make effective communication where they express themselves and look to iron things out. This general inability to communicate puts a wedge in the possibility of a dialogue. The reason being that for dialogue to occur, effective communication must take place.

In turn, dialogue is a compulsory component of dispute management because for two people to arrive at a solution, they must be willing to talk to and hear each other out honestly and without bias. Only then would they be able to find common ground that appeals to them and sort out the differences between them with objectiveness and unity. Otherwise, any form of communication between them would be no less of a debate, with each partner looking to outdo the other. Listening thus becomes an activity primed at picking out points for an argument rather than for attentiveness. That is, when communication is nonexistent or wrongly done in a relationship, partners would listen to each other for the purpose of debating rather than listening to understand or derive meaning. And as it is in debates, it is impossible for both parties to arrive at a solution or common ground. One party would be the victor, and the other vanquished.

### *Inability to confide in one another (this destroys the balance of the couple)*

To confide in someone means being able to share secrets with the person. In other words, it means being able to discuss personal or sensitive information with a person. For someone to be your confidant — the one whom you confide in — you and that person need to have a good rapport. Rapport is a relationship based on mutually held respect and trust. In turn, to build a rapport with someone, you both have to have an effective system of communication from which trust and respect are built over time.

Logically, it is somewhat irrational to confide in someone you hardly or are unable to speak to. Thus, when you and your partner have a wrongly based or nonexistent system of communication, confiding in one another is going to be difficult if not impossible. If you have experienced something of this sort when you or your partner avoid each other, choosing instead to go to other sources to be heard out, chances are wrong or nonexistent communication is responsible. As such, you find out you both find it relatively easier talking about things to a person with whom you have a good rapport like a parent, sibling, or friend. So, whatever comes up, be it a fight, dispute, or a sensitive issue, you end up shutting yourself out from your partner to go open up to a third party. The inability to confide in your partner means you end up outsourcing solutions to problems in your relationship to foreign parties because you and partner are unable to have effective communication in which you sort out your issues. In the end, this complication can cause couples to feel out of balance with each other, thus, accounting for why they would look outside the relationship for support.

### Solitude

When a couple has a nonexistent or wrong system of communication, they have trouble having substantial dialogues. Conversely, the lack of dialogue over time means that the couple grow separately. The reason being that communication is an integral part of the bonding process and being unable to grow and maintain that connection through communication implies that the bond would wane over time.

With the right and effective communication system, every relationship is similar to creeper plants which when planted at the same time, grow upwards entwining each other to form thicker and stronger bunches in the process. Conversely, when a wrong or nonexistent communication system is introduced into a relationship like allowing a third-party intrusion, it is like placing planting sticks between creepers. The creepers grow upwards entwining the sticks rather than each other. In the end, the creepers grow in solitude, therefore becoming more exposed and vulnerable in the process. The same applies to relationships. Once both partners drift apart and begin to grow on their own, the relationship becomes susceptible to all manner of crises.

**Immediate closure**

If you and your partner can barely strike up an effective conversation, you will find it relatively easier to avoid bringing up certain issues and would want them to be gone rather than actually bringing them up for discussion. The reason for this act of being closed off to your partner can stem from a variety of reasons, such as the ones outlined below:

**The fear of judgment**

Being unable to talk to someone involves being unable to decipher how the person would react. Consider this narrative in the communication system of a couple; when you and your partner operate a wrong or nonexistent communication system, you would be afraid of bringing up certain discussions for fear of being judged. The reason being that you are unable to accurately assume their perspective and judgments. As such, to avoid being judged, you would just about suppress any urge to strike up a conversation.

**The fear of rejection**

Like in the case of judgment, the fear of being rejected by your partner because of the poor communication system between you both can make you bottle up your emotions and become closed off to your partner. This is even more pronounced when you are a particularly sensitive and emotional person. There is a level of wariness even after you have decided to open up to your partner. This is as a result of not being able to determine what response you would get upon sharing your thoughts with them. This is why many of such people — the really sensitive kinds — prefer to bottle up their emotions and put up a front, rather than take that leap of faith and talk to their partner.

**Inability to understand your partner's feelings**

The only reason you would be unable to understand what your partner feels is a sign that the communication system between you is either wrong or nonexistent. Have you observed that you sometimes predict the reactions of people to certain subjects, mirror some of their traits, and learn of the emotions they typically exhibit when you communicate frequently? The same should apply to a relationship where communication is effective. Otherwise, you may find it difficult to understand what your partner feels at some point.

This can be detrimental to the relationship because it would make you seem insensitive and difficult to understand. Also, you may wind up bringing up subjects that your partner is highly sensitive to without knowing. This can cause your partner to repress their emotions and adopt closed character behavior.

## Chapter 4: The Six Most Common Mistakes in Communication to Avoid

When it comes to communication, we often get it wrong more times than right. Worse than that is how clueless we can be about why we were misunderstood or not listened to. Communication, as we have learned at this point, is a vital part of romantic relationships. As such, we must become mindful of the mistakes we inadvertently make in communication and take responsibility for those that are deliberate. Below are the six most common mistakes.

## You Don't Listen to Your Partner When They Speak

Sometimes, it isn't about providing a solution to whatever issues they might have. Merely listening when they tell you what weighs heavily on their mind tells them that you care. It is also a sign of respect that you have for your partner and the relationship you both have committed to. Truly listening is not about sitting and pretending to be attentive. There are quite a few things that you must keep in mind to do.

### Be Empathetic

When anyone speaks about emotional intelligence — the single factor that many successful leaders are credited with — they will always talk about empathy. But, what exactly is empathy and why is this important?

46

Simply put, it is the ability to stand where the other person is and feel exactly what they are trying to express in words. This is in contrast to sympathy, which is being able to feel sorry for what the person is going through. Going by this definition, it is clear which is the most effective at getting people to believe that you are truly listening. No one is born gifted with empathy, we all have a responsibility to develop it. It is a conscious effort to relate with your partner's feelings, even when you did not physically experience what you are being told.

When you are empathetic, you may convey this with a hug or by saying things in line with what your partner is talking about that show you are not detached.

### Don't Interrupt

When it comes to that seemingly justifiable and near irresistible urge to point something out when your partner is talking to you, you should ignore it. It can feel right and appropriate, but it might come off to your partner as you not really being interested in what they have to say. Regardless of how incoherent or irrational what you're being told might seem, you ought to let them get it off their chest without cutting them off.

When you are talking to your partner, you must keep in mind that you are not in a debate. Tame your impatience. Many times, what people may have to say, if we only let them finish, tend to change the course and tone of the entire conversation. Holding your tongue for a few minutes more could let you look in hindsight and be thankful you did not jeer at your partner, have an outburst, or cut them off.

### Be Careful with Unsolicited Advice

While it is not necessarily wrong to give advice to your partner when you think they need it, you should be careful to only do so when it is asked. Sometimes, all your partner needs from you is a listening ear. You should be able to do just that without dishing out from your well of wisdom and experience.

If you feel that you must give them advice, then be courteous in your approach to it. You absolutely do not want to appear like a know-it-all to your partner. Ask if it is alright that you give them advice concerning that particular issue and see if it is welcomed.

### Appreciate Different Communication Styles

As simple as the topic of communication might seem to you, it is a lot more complex than that. Have you ever heard two people who, although are making the same points essentially, cannot seem to agree? They might argue for hours without knowing that they are on the same side. This is why listening is so important. It helps you to know your partner better and understand where they are coming from.

There are certain styles of communication that must be known as they affect the outcome of any conversation. They include;

- **Passive communication**: With this style, the communicator tries to avoid conflict and is more agreeable than necessary. They speak without passion and may be misunderstood because they can sometimes come across as indifferent. It is, by some people, referred to as the submissive method of communication. This is because passive communicators would much prefer to give in to the demands of others just to avoid confrontational or conflict situations. You will also find them being very apologetic people, even when they are clearly in the right.

- **Manipulative communication**: Manipulators like to choose and time their words with care. They are cunning, deceptive, and may seek to cause harm to their partners for their own selfish benefits. But they do this so shrewdly, that they rarely ever appear to be destructive. There are usually deliberate undertones to the words they speak, which convey a different meaning than is obvious. They are also quite good at making others feel sorry for what they shouldn't and then end up acting against their better judgement.

- **Aggressive communication**: These kinds of communicators may be loud and threatening in the way they express their feelings. They make demands and the rationality or kindness of their points may be lost in the intimidating nature of their approach. The aggressive communicator might imagine themselves to be close to perfection (if not perfect) and would usually ascribe the blame for every failure in their lives to others besides themselves. They are often preoccupied with getting their way to see things from a win-win perspective. While they may appear a little similar to manipulative communicators, their methods are often brash and direct — this is opposed to the more subtle and cunning style characterized by manipulators.

- **Assertive communication**: This is often declared as the best way to converse with anyone. Especially, your partner in a relationship. This is because assertiveness is not selfish. It aims for a win-win. Assertive communicators try to explain and discuss their feelings, hurt or not, without blaming their partners. Those who are assertive try to do the best they can for people but are never hesitant to say no when they need to. They can be empathetic but will also speak about their own emotions and needs without shame. They take responsibility for the results they experience, whether positive or negative, and will often look straight at whoever they are speaking with.

- **Passive-aggressive communication**: An analogy for this is anger bottled up and labeled with a smiley face. Such communicators may act unconcerned and lackadaisical, but one can often tell that they are steaming beneath the surface. Their body language and the expressions on their face with these kinds of communicators should not be trusted as an accurate picture of their true emotions. The silent treatment is the most common method used by passive-aggressive communicators.

### *Couples Therapy*

If your partner has been on your case for a while to see a therapist about the ineffective or non-existent communication in your relationship, you should take them seriously. If they haven't, then you should suggest it to them. Whichever name you prefer to call it, therapy or counseling, the fact remains that it is one of the best and safest places to air out your relationship issues and help you learn how to listen to your partner.

Before any advice is given at all by the counselor, you can observe how they give you complete attention without interrupting or debating you while you speak. There's nothing better than having someone who is experienced at handling different kinds of relationship problems and has a balanced opinion of you and your partner, guide you through all the little (yet highly crucial) things you have missed.

### *Make Your Partner a Priority*

Nothing else should matter when your partner is trying to share their thoughts with you. If you are too caught up in other activities to give them your full attention, then it is better to tell them and arrange a different time to have that conversation. Otherwise, you should put everything aside to listen. Quick glances to check what's going on in the kitchen or keeping up with the news update on your newspaper or the television will just show you find what your partner is sharing with you insignificant.

You should sit facing them, maintain eye contact, and catch every word and inflection as they speak. You can stop them if you missed what they had just said and would like that they repeat themselves. Otherwise, focus your mind on listening without speaking.

### *Think*

To truly listen, you must also process what is being said. Mull it over with an open mind. Take in every word that is spoken to you ponder them. By so doing, your response will have a more positive impact on your partner.

In keeping an open mind, here are some tips to guide you;

1. Understand that people will often have differing opinions from you. You cannot always expect them to agree with you on everything. In fact, the relationship will be more enjoyable when you are with someone who is not afraid to challenge your opinions constructively and speak their mind freely. Do not see people as inferior because they express a different perspective than yours. Listen to them and try to see the reason in their opinions. Who knows, you might end up agreeing with them.

2. Don't guess what your partner is trying to say or look for deeper meaning into their words. Let them clarify themselves. This does not only include vocal speculations. You should also avoid coming to your own conclusions in your mind. If there was anything you missed while they were talking, ask that they repeat themselves. Share your understanding of all they had said to avoid misinterpretation. If certain things were not said or alluded to, don't attempt to read the mind of your partner.

3. Many times, our minds are involuntarily closed. We may have been accepting of our partner's opinions but were too distracted to even listen. Keep your focus on your partner. Otherwise, you might end up with all the wrong conclusions after you have missed some vital points of the conversation.

4. Try not to let biases of any kind color your vision of your partner. They are human beings like yourself with personal opinions, flaws, and so on. For some closed-minded people in relationships, the problem is that they think their partner's opinions are without substance and entirely reliant on what religion they subscribe to or the popular opinion on a particular topic. Give people the benefit of the doubt. If you must make

any assumptions about your partner's viewpoint, let it be that it is unbiased, rational, and intelligent.

Some benefits of open-mindedness are;

1.  People will return the favor and listen to you. What is the point of having smart and helpful things to say, if no one will pay you any mind? Granted, some folks may continue to be closed-minded. But, for the most part, you would have more active listeners.

2.  Your life would flourish. This is common for people who remain open to new ideas and opportunities. They have a better chance at success. This is because of the growth that comes with being open-minded. It is said that one's best assets are the people in their lives. Individuals who do not immediately shoot down others who share different opinions from them tend to have more friends and people who easily rely on and turn to them.

3.  Open-mindedness would make for a fun person to be around. People would be comfortable to share their thoughts with you and you would have a lot more to say in your conversations. You add to your knowledge bank every time you take in a point of view that is new to you. Open-mindedness also tends to lead to the development of other fine qualities. Such qualities include ingenuity and originality.

4.  A closed-minded person may shy away from new challenges. By so doing, they would lack the necessary confidence needed to thrive in trying situations. Usually, they look for a comfortable or familiar way to go about things and stick to it even when more effective methods are presented to them. They do not

explore or push the boundaries of their potential and thus, do not grow.

5.  There is a definite association between open-mindedness and creativity. People who are closed-minded about any subject will, very likely, not question their previously held beliefs on it. As such, you will find that many of these people are neither dreamers nor explorers; two hallmarks of a creative person. The open-minded individual learns the possibilities in new ideas and is not afraid to give them a try if the positives outweigh the negatives. According to Walt Disney, you must first be able to imagine a thing before you can set out to create it. And what chance has the imagination to fly when the mind is closed shut?

## *Respect*

If you already hold little regard for your partner, their opinions would have an even smaller stature, and it isn't much of an incentive to spend time listening to opinions you feel have no importance or are beneath you. This is why ideas like love at first sight or a whirlwind romance is not a good enough basis for any relationship. For such unions to survive the usual hurdles that are often faced by romantic relationships, both parties must have mutual respect. The importance and necessity of respect are non-negotiable for couples.

If your partner has ever accused you of not showing them respect or you worry that you are being disrespected in your relationship, below are some behaviors that, when noticed, could prove that you and your partner have some work to do in your relationship, especially when it concerns the issue of respect.

- We all have those habits which cannot go with us into a relationship. They may be fine to us, but others might not be able to tolerate them for too long. Feelings of love may not be enough of an incentive to change these aspects of ourselves. The respect you have for your partner, and one that you also expect in turn, is sure to do the trick. Say you have always complained about how your partner prefers to leave their dirty clothes in a disorderly manner in the room. Should they continue to do so without making even the slightest effort towards changing, this is a sign of disrespect.

- If you notice that your partner is only partially present when you are talking to them, it could be that they have a very small opinion of you, and vice versa. In a relationship, no one involved should have to beg for attention. Both parties should be interested in each other enough to want to listen.

- How many times have you caught your partner lying to you and then forgave them, only for that person to do it again and again? While they might try to paint it as a good thing, saying that they tell you lies to save the relationship or because they love and respect you, this is not a fact. When one is honest with their partner and works on changing certain things about themselves to avoid lying in the future, these are definite signs of respect. Understandably, some people might react to the truth in a manner that suggests they would much prefer a lie. Still, you should respect yourself and the relationship enough to keep your promise of honesty.

- For any healthy relationship to prosper, both parties must set their boundaries at the onset. It becomes the duty of both partners in the relationship to not cross the lines they had agreed to. To intentionally breach this agreement shows that the offending partner may not respect the other. It doesn't matter how ridiculous the set boundaries are or what aspects of the relationship they concern, what is important is that you and your partner agreed to them.

- While this may be a fear of commitment more than a sign of disrespect, it is possible that your partner refuses to go with you to family meetings because they have little or no respect for you. That is, they don't care about how important it is to you that they meet your family. You should ask them about this. Making a relationship work is no easy business. Sometimes, difficult sacrifices must be made. If after discussing with them, they have nothing to say as to why they don't want to meet your family, it just might be a problem of respect.

- Unless there was another agreement made by both partners, an unspoken rule of most relationships is exclusivity. As such, both partners must respect each other's feelings enough to not kiss, fondle, sext, or make love to other people. It is no secret the things that are forbidden in exclusive relationships. To do them anyway is disrespectful and can be really hurtful.

- If your partner's feelings count for nothing with you, then you will not think much about making hurtful jokes at their expense, especially in public. You should be on their side rooting for and defending them. Granted, we all make mistakes and might do things to offend our partners. But if you do not feel sorry for your actions, or if your partner does not apologize to you, then you need no other sign to recognize this blatant lack of respect.

### Bad Listening Habits

There are certain habits that are common in many people which prevent us from truly listening when we are spoken to. One of them is rehearsing your reply. This may happen when you believe you know what your partner is getting at and are only waiting for them to stop talking. Another is a stubborn conviction that you are right. In such situations, it matters very little what is said as it will unlikely change your mind. Your mind would shut out all rationality. Have you ever found yourself daydreaming while someone is speaking to you? It happens more often than you think. It further stresses the point that listening is conscious and deliberate. You must make an effort to keep your mind in the here and now.

### Eye Contact

Look directly at your partner while they are speaking. This is not to say that you must stare uncomfortably into their eyes without once changing your focus. But, frequently maintaining eye contact and consciously looking at them shows that you are present. Even though we do not mean to, many of us are guilty of getting distracted when our partners need our attention most. Your partner is probably not going to like you checking your social media messages at the same time they are talking to you. Such behaviors might lead them to conclude that their thoughts and emotions mean little or nothing to you.

### *Show That You Are Attentive*

Giving your partner signs that your focus has not shifted from them may not seem like much, but it is ingrained in us to look out for proof of attentiveness when we are conversing with anyone. Nodding, repeating what was heard, and ah-hahs are some proofs that you are present in the conversation. When you do these, your partner is encouraged to relax and continue speaking. Their confidence that they are being heard is reinforced, and they appreciate you more for it. Besides occasionally repeating some of what your partner said, you may summarize all their thoughts back to them to ensure you heard right and assure your partner that they haven't just wasted their time.

## You Are Often Complaining About Something

One reason why you fail to successfully communicate your thoughts to your partner is because they sound like complaints. While it isn't wrong to speak about your hurt feelings or how you were wronged, you should learn to forgive, stop talking about the same issue (even after it has been resolved), and understand that no one likes a whiner. But did you know that complaining can affect your health?

For one, whining about a situation will stress you and your partner out rather than solve the problem, and it is no new discovery that stress impairs your immune system in more ways than you can afford. While it is nearly impossible to avoid feeling stressed at some point in our lives, constantly putting yourself in such situations is a danger to your health. Stress can affect aspects including fertility, mental health, blood sugar levels, sex drive, and the heart (Legg, 2017). Some symptoms of stress include headaches, insomnia, and restlessness. Your relationship is also at risk when you constantly drag it down with frequent complaints.

More dangers of complaining include;

- **Fatigue**: As already stated, complaining causes one to feel stressed. Although high amounts of energy are produced and released while the individual is complaining, tiredness almost immediately sets in once they are done. Should they sustain this period of cortisol and adrenaline release for too long, they would feel so drained at the end that they might not feel motivated or energetic enough to do other activities.

- **Even more stress**: This is what often happens. It's like a snowball effect on the body, where getting stressed by complaining only increases your stress levels. There are few ways to better vividly remember what happened to you than talking about it. But simply discussing the matter with someone is healthy. Lamenting about the issue and seeking sympathy is something that should be consciously avoided.

- **Mood killing**: Complaining is a definite mood killer for everyone involved. It is unlikely that you will feel good afterwards and your partner's mood may be dampened. Also, you may start with worry and end up with feelings of anger or sadness. Complaining to your partner may cause them to feel stressed too. And, as already discussed, this is not good for their mental or physical health.

- **Creativity blocker**: Creativity is a necessary skill for problem-solving. Why, you ask? Because it directs our focus away the problem to find a solution. Instead of complaining about how rough life has been and all the things that are not going right, you can be imaginative and figure out a path in a seemingly daunting situation. Complaining is an effective way to stunt your creative process.

- **Anxiety**: Although pessimism is seen by some as the best way to view life (in their opinion, you will be less disappointed). In reality, viewing life through the lens of negativity will cause you to feel less confident and more anxious. It exaggerates the seriousness of the situation and could lead to depression. Complaining is usually a pessimist's way of dealing with problems. They discuss the negativity and intensify the problem.

- **Relationship breaker**: Your partner might indeed want to be there for you. But repeatedly complaining can feel boring and laborious. Constantly feeling pity for yourself and wanting your partner to take time off whatever they could be doing and join your pity party may cause them to stop spending time with you. They would also be wary to have conversations with you, as it might lead to another session of your complaints. This distance and bad communication weakens any relationship, regardless of how justifiable the complaints are or the amount of love professed.

Instead of moping and feeling like no one has it worse than you, here are a few healthy alternatives;

- **Thankfulness**: When you are dealt a bad hand in life, as will often happen to each one of us at some point, you always have two choices: sulk or rise up to the challenge. Choosing the latter is most definitely the better and more productive option. One way to make it easier to face any challenge head-on is through gratitude. There is so much to be grateful for, if you spend time thinking about it. For one, being alive means that you've still got a chance at success. Be grateful for friends, family, or the fact that you are reading this book right now. The mental switch from being a complainer to a thankful person may be all you need.

- **Selflessness**: This is not to say that you should completely take yourself out of the picture. The thing is, complaints are usually from a place of selfishness. For example, you are always thinking about yourself and your own problems that you become oblivious to the fact that your partner is also going through issues or they may be losing patience with your incessant complaining.

- **Forgiveness**: Learn to forgive quickly. Of course, it is no easy feat to forgive someone when they have cheated, betrayed, or wronged us in some way. Still, forgiveness is too important to not give it a try or, at least, consider. Once you have truly forgiven anyone — including yourself — you will find less need to complain about whatever happened. Indeed, forgiveness does more for the person who let's go, than who is forgiven. You may have heard this before, but it stands as the truth: you cannot control the actions of others. The best you can do is trust and hope for the best in people. When they betray that trust, you can choose to forgive. This is something you *can* control.

When you are able to forgive, you can help others follow the same path. And isn't that a good thing? Instead of complaining and draining your partner, you can add value to their lives and earn their respect.

- **A deeper resolve**: Take, for example, a man who has tried many times to get a business to work or to find a job. Repeated failure can make one feel down and sad, but merely complaining every time it happens in no way solves the problem. This man could decide to do things differently. Instead of wasting his energy and feeling depressed and drained, he could learn from his failures and use the hurt and anger as fuel. He could become even more determined to achieve their goals and reevaluate his previous methods. Complaining does nothing good for you or your partner, and it is harmful to communication. Resolve is admirable and a step forward.

## You Feel Superior to Your Partner

It is not unheard of in many failing relationships that one person thinks of themselves as better than their partners. In reality, this is never true. Usually, it is narcissism unchecked. These individuals refuse to believe that their partner complements them in some way and may talk down to them. This delusion of absolute superiority is destructive to communication in relationships. The individual could feel that they are smarter and more experienced than their partners and would prefer to speak than listen.

### Some Easily Identifiable Signs of Narcissism

- They are very critical of certain character traits in people which, on close observation, can in found in them. They will often refuse to accept that they also behave in the same manner they condemn. They might vehemently deny their faults, while they focus on those of others.

- Opinions which do not agree with those of a narcissistic partner are met with rude, angry, and brash behavior. They do not take kindly to opposing viewpoints. The narcissist is happiest when others nod and cheer in agreement as they express what they believe is the best and smartest idea. They might get into a wild rage if the impracticality of their ideas is pointed out. This may be because there are more serious issues hidden beneath the superiority complex: guilt, shame, and fear for example (Seltzer, 2013). As such, revealing faults in their ideas, personality, or abilities may unearth those hidden emotions. They would lash out in an attempt to protect themselves.

- They, quite often, do not know when to stop before they are encroaching upon someone else's boundaries. Earlier, we discussed that boundaries must be set before the relationship begins. A narcissist might agree to such terms but would eventually not respect it. As dark as it may seem, narcissists tend to see other people as mere tools to be used as they please. They also do not understand the concept of selflessness. When they do their partners a favor, they expect that a favor for them be returned sometime in the future. They might start conversations without seeking their partner's consent and, in some cases, cannot be trusted to keep a secret — not even their own.

- You may have inferred from the above points that the narcissist is usually not empathetic. Well, that is exactly true. Their only concern is for themselves and everyone else is just a means to an end. This includes their partners. The only time they would show care is when the needs of their partners match their own. You cannot simply expect the narcissist to place themselves in your shoes when they are stuck in their own heads.

- They are often bullies in relationships, and you will find them telling their partners how they should be more like them. A relationship blossoms when both parties embrace the team player spirit. For narcissists, their relationships are also merely tools for their personal and selfish gains. They expect a lot and rarely, if ever, give in return. They often make demands and ensure they have their way either by the use of physical force or through manipulative techniques.

- They find it hard to be sincerely happy for the success of their partners. Sometimes, they pretend to be. But other times, the envy in their eyes and body language is undeniable. They want to be the ones celebrated at all times and are often in competition with their partners. Many times, such partners are unaware of this silent competition. But their feeling of envy does not end there. Narcissists are usually very driven people and, as such, are likely to experience career success. When this happens, they might become paranoid in thinking others, including their partners, are envious of them. They might convince themselves that certain people are out to get them and would cut out long-time friends and loved ones from their lives. They would get suspicious of their partners and start keeping secrets.

- While this may not exactly be true for all narcissists, some of them have a firm belief in the exceptional brilliance of their minds and are convinced that that they are "special". They prefer to keep company with those they consider of high intellect or social standing. They are also very picky about who they choose to get into a relationship with. They have an ideal picture of how that person looks, talks, dresses, and even the kind of job they have. And since it is unlikely they would find people who fit this mental picture perfectly, their relationships are often toxic.

- They are some of the haughtiest people you will ever come across — or get into a relationship with. Since they believe you need them but they don't need you, they behave arrogantly and do nothing to ensure the stability of the relationship. They often never seek the forgiveness of their partners, regardless of the grievousness of their actions, but they would demand the apology of those who commit even the slightest of errors. They believe they are entitled to the good things in life not as a result of how hard they have worked for it, but because of how special and better they are in comparison to others.

### You Can Change as a Narcissist

Although, the popular opinion about narcissists is that this character is like the spots on a leopard, it is not factually accurate. While they cannot change their narcissism in itself, the behavioral patterns associated with it can be controlled. Narcissists *can* change their high-minded, self-centered, and manipulative ways to be more empathetic and humble. If it struck you from the points listed above that you might be a narcissist or have some narcissistic traits, you don't have to let it ruin your relationship.

But, without willingness on your part, there really is little hope of salvaging your relationship from the claws of narcissism. The first step, as you probably already know, is to acknowledge and accept the fact that you have this disorder. If you suspect your partner is a narcissist, then understand that appealing to their guilt or seeking empathy from them would only yield futility - they do things for themselves and because of themselves, it has little or nothing to do with you. Also, their narcissistic behaviors are more so habits than calculated actions. It has become an indistinguishable part of their character over time.

So, how then can you make a narcissist change their unhealthy behavioral patterns? The answer is consequences. When the narcissist is faced with the potential loss of something they care about, then they could force themselves into breaking that pattern. In one example, a woman whose spouse was a physically abusive narcissist purchased a dog who helped her husband stop the habit of hitting her. Although the dog was not taken home for this purpose, it grew up to be a large dog and would attack the husband whenever he started hitting her. With time, the narcissist husband stopped abusing his wife and, even after the dog died, did not return to his habit (The Little Shaman, 2018). Some can also achieve this change in the behaviors of their narcissist partner by threatening to leave the relationship should they continue with certain patterns. Remember, the narcissist's only concern is for themselves. As such, they must care a lot about the consequences to dislike their narcissistic behaviors, in order for them to put a stop to it. If they don't feel motivated enough to stop they will just find a reason to continue, and your pleas, blames, and so on would count for very little with them.

Two things are very important here. First, there should be a consequence that means something to the narcissist. Secondly, the individual must dislike their characteristic narcissistic actions and want to change. For the change to happen, both internal and external factors must be in place.

66

There are definitely other ways to go about changing the harmful behaviors of a narcissist, but employing consequences is the most effective.

## You Continuously Point Out What Your Partner is Doing Wrong

Fault-finding usually seems like harmless constructive criticism, but repeatedly pointing out your partner's errors will weaken and eventually break your relationship. No one has or will ever be able to attain a state of total perfection in body, personality, and so on. This is because we all want different things from people and define "perfect" differently. What you see as abominable may be considered by another beautiful and just right.

Consistently looking for errors in your partner will make them feel embarrassed and like they aren't valuable to you. Your conversation with your partner shouldn't always be about blame, and if you must make their errors known to them, do it patiently and with love. Do not raise your voice at them or use yourself as a perfect example they should live up to. We have already discussed the effects of disrespect in relationships. Frequent fault-finding reveals a lack of respect. It also adversely affects your partner's self-confidence as they begin to see themselves as incompetent and unworthy. This could lead them to act out by no longer trying to change certain behaviors they know are harmful.

If that is not enough to get you to stop nitpicking, you should know that this behavior also affects your life negatively. Some of the dangers of fault-finding are coldness in the relationship, depression, and even the death of some cells in your body (Kushnick, 2015).

67

Instead of nitpicking, you should learn to look beyond certain behaviors. Be more accepting and do away with your expectations of perfection. No one is made to fit such a mold.

## You Try to Read Your Partner's Mind

This is not meant in the same sense as telepathy or the likes. But, we are often culprits of coming to conclusions and judgments before the person talking to us even finishes their thoughts. As a result, we make the wrong inferences and get into unnecessary and avoidable quarrels with our partner. Remember to always let people finish their points before cutting in with what you believe they were about to say.

Also, we attempt to read the minds of our partners through their body language. As such, you would believe yourself capable of telling, for example, when they are sad and what exactly is responsible for the sadness. Or they could be unusually silent one day, and you come to the conclusion that it must be about you.

Communication in your relationship is about letting and listening to your partner speak their mind. Not just that, but they should do so in their own way and at their own pace. When they are done, you must make sure both of you are in agreement with what they were trying to say before saying anything else.

Many times, the problem is mostly solved by letting your partner speak. There is a level of satisfaction experienced when one is allowed to voice their thoughts. Also, you would better understand them and know what to say or do in response.

## You Make Jokes at the Expense of Your Partner

Having a sense of humor is not a bad thing. In fact, it is considered a very attractive quality by many. The problem is when one partner tries to be funny at the expense of the other party. Then, it leaves the realm of comedy and becomes ridicule. This is also why communication and a good understanding of your partner is important. Sometimes, the ridiculed partner may choose to hide the fact that they were offended by a particular joke. They might even play along and pretend to find what was said to be funny.

Without knowing it, they have rewarded and encouraged this behavior in their partner, and like little kids, such a reward results in the repetition of the act. They would continue to publicly and privately demean you.

But that is assuming the ridiculing isn't done on purpose. Some partners can be manipulative to the point of disguising barbed insults as mere jokes just for laughs. They might enjoy the discomfort that is displayed by their partner when they poke fun at them. You must determine which of the two your partner is: the manipulator or the funny one.

By so doing, you can determine which course of action to take. Sit with them and calmly discuss how it hurts you when they make jokes about certain things and in certain places. Define your boundaries to them and be observant as you speak to them. If your partner is immediately regretful and refrains from such humor in the future, this is a good sign. Otherwise, you might have to consider breaking it off with such a person. There is no worthy enough reason for you to endure this kind of relationship. And no, the fact that others find it funny does not excuse disrespect. The fact that it breaks you down means it must stop. An example of this veiled verbal abuse is when they expose your insecurities and errors to people outside your relationship.

## Chapter 5: Strategies to Improve Couple's Communication

In every relationship, particularly romantic relationships, communication is very important. This is one truth that has been heavily elaborated upon by many writers over the years; however, it does appear as though even with a large amount of information regarding communication in relationships, a lot of people do not know how to improve communication with their partners. One reason includes the advent of social media; partners hardly have time to have physical conversations about issues affecting them. Another reason is that a lot of couples do not understand how exactly communication – or the lack of it – impacts their relationships. Finally, one of the reasons couples fail miserably in the art of communication is because of the fact that they lack the knowledge of how they can improve their communication skills with their partners.

When there is a lack of understanding on how important communication is to your relationship, you have to first understand that communication is the only way your partner can get an insight into what you are thinking. Unless he/she is a clairvoyant, there is no way you can expect them to know what you are thinking and understand how you feel about certain issues, especially when you have misgivings about certain actions of theirs and want them to change. Thus, an understanding of the importance of communication in your relationship is a good way to solve many problems in relationships.

If, on the other hand, you do not have issues with understanding the importance of communication is in a relationship, but rather, you do not know what strategies to employ to improve communication between yourself and your partner, then you are in the right place. In this chapter of the book, I will be discussing the actions you could take if you want to improve communication with your partner and reap the rewards that come out of a robust communication system.

One of the tips include setting out a particular time and location to speak with your partner. It should be somewhere away from noise and distraction. When communicating with your partner, they should be the focus of the conversation so you should make sure you are not distracted by family, friends, or your phone! Also, when trying to communicate something specific, for instance, when you are attempting to inform your partner about a particular behavioral trait that you do not appreciate, you need to make it as specific as possible; do not sound confrontational and do not make it about the general 'bad behavior' of the person. In this sort of scenario, you should talk about the specific action and how it affects you. During conversations, always be willing to meet your partner halfway. Bear in mind that you do not have to be right. In fact, in these sorts of situations, it seldom matters who is right. The important thing is that there is an amicable resolution of whatever conflict it is that has arisen, and for that to be possible, you need to learn how to compromise.

Finally, on this note, part of having a great conversation includes the ability to listen to your partner. In seeking to understand your partner better, listening is quite important. Listening lets the other party know that they are being heard and that whatever they have to say is valid and is of importance to you. In this regard, they are more open to listening to you and getting feedback. If you want to improve your listening skills, you should begin by trying not to interrupt your partner while they are speaking. Maintain eye contact with them and maintain a posture that suggests that you are open to whatever it is your partner has to say. Create an atmosphere that makes your partner comfortable, within which they can be honest and open to you regarding whatever issues they are having.

Now that we are done with discussing the specific steps you could take in improving communication with your partner, we will quickly look at the specific steps one can take in order to make sure that communication with their partner is top-notch.

## *Use "I" statements instead of "You" statements*

This is very important, especially if you are pointing out something your partner is doing wrong or a trait that you do not entirely like. People often get defensive in these sorts of situations, especially when they feel they are being attacked or cornered. Using "You" statements makes it sound accusatory, as though you are indicting your partner for whatever failings it is that you are seeking to rectify. So, when this is the case, it is better to just make the focus on you instead of your partner. So instead of saying, "You often misunderstand what I say." You could rephrase it and say, "Perhaps I am not often clear when sharing my thoughts…"

When you choose this route, you offer your partner the opportunity to admit their errors and subsequently make amends. Using "I" statements can be a way of deflecting a potentially tense situation. Of course, it does not suggest that you will be taking responsibility for the failings of your partner. When you employ the technique effectively, you will still be able to communicate to your partner what it is about their actions you do not like. They will still realize they are wrong. The difference in the two approaches – i.e. calling them out with "You" statements and gently pointing out the errors using "I" statements – is that in the latter there is room for the partner to acknowledge the existence of the problem and to make amends.

### Ask questions

It is possible that in a relationship, one partner does all of the talking. This could be because this partner feels quite comfortable getting their thoughts together and letting them out, or because they are more in charge/aware of themselves in the relationship than the other party. Whatever the reason is, it is often unhealthy if only one party does all of the talking in a relationship.

No communication has happened if only one person does the talking and the other party is not involved. Communication is a two-way street, which means that there is a mutual sharing of thoughts and feelings between the two parties, so any time you realize that your partner is not saying as much as they could, you should get them to start talking. One of the ways to get your partner comfortable enough to begin to open up is through asking questions.

Your partner may not feel comfortable talking for a variety of reasons. Perhaps they are timid, or maybe they just want to listen and not contribute, or they may have just gotten used to you doing all the talking and so just leave the conversation up to you. These latter reasons may seem romantic, but they are actually harmful to your relationship. You need to know what your partner thinks about certain things at some point, so it is essential that you get them to talk.

Asking questions, particularly open-ended questions, give your partner the opportunity to talk. When this is done consistently over time, they will get comfortable with the idea of sharing their thoughts and before long will begin to take the initiative themselves. When you ask open-ended questions, you give your partner room to go beyond what you asked them and venture into other areas. For instance, when you ask, "How was your day?" your partner can choose to talk about a variety of things within this context. If they really want to talk and have been looking for the perfect opportunity, asking them an open-ended question is an excellent way to get the ball rolling.

When you are dealing with a partner who is unfamiliar with the process of sharing their thoughts, you need to have a lot of patience. The first few times that you ask them questions, they may not be as forthcoming as you would like; however, you need to give them room to grow. Eventually, they will get to the point where they would no longer need any coaxing from you or anybody else before they start sharing their thoughts and feelings. But while they are still at this stage, give them all the room they need to grow.

***Touch and smile – this creates intimacy and is more than just about the sex***

A lot of times we underestimate non-verbal communication. We take it for granted that a lot can be said without a single word said between the couple. One of the greatest non-verbal ways that partners can communicate is through touch. It shows a level of intimacy if a partner can just touch the other without saying anything. In that single moment, a lot is passed between the couple.

You may not know it, but your partner may be craving your touch, especially if they are going through a tough time and need some form of assurance or validation. When your partner is going through trying times, simply holding their hand or giving them a tap on the shoulder could be all they need to pull through that situation. Also, when you have just had a fight with your partner, touch could be your own way of seeking to mend the relationship. Even in the instances where the fault is theirs, your touch could be a way to tell them that you are seeking to mend the relationship. It makes it easier for them to take the olive branch and to move on with the relationship at that point.

Sharing a touch can also be a way to increase intimacy with your partner. Sharing a touch is like having a secret language with your partner, and that can help to increase the privacy shared by the two of you. You must understand that intimacy does not necessarily refer to sex, although, of course, it may be possible that sharing a touch can end up in sex. Intimacy connotes a situation where a feeling of closeness and attachment is shared between you and your partner in the relationship. Sex is taken to be one of the major drivers of intimacy. However, apart from sex, partners can increase their intimacy in a variety of ways, sharing a touch can be one of them.

### Ask yourself what you can do

Every healthy relationship is one where both partners bring something to the table. If you always rely on your partner to initiate intimacy and keep the relationship going, then you only show that you are a selfish person with no intention of seeing the relationship grow. Thus, instead of looking for ways through which your partner can make the relationship work more efficiently, you should be asking yourself what you can contribute to the relationship to get it moving to the next stage.

Thus, when you are beginning a relationship, always go with the mindset that you will be contributing from your own quota to make sure that the relationship works out. You should not wait for the relationship to fall apart before you start looking for a way to resuscitate it.

You can also ask your partner what they would want you to do. You may be surprised at the things they request, especially concerning the relationship. When asking these questions, be genuine in your request for an answer. Do not perform an action because someone else did it, or because it has become the fashionable thing to do. While asking your partner of what you can do in the relationship, be sure that you have made up your mind to carry out the actions demanded by your partner because it would be your way of saying that you value and respect the relationship. It is only in exceptional cases that you can decide not to carry out the request of your partner. This is in situations where it would be a detriment to you to do the things requested by your partner. But even at that, you still need to offer explanations to your partner as to why you could not carry out their request.

Furthermore, you can also decide to take the initiative to surprise your partner. You can figure out what they want, and you can try to make that available even without your partner requesting for it. This does not just refer to physical items or possessions; you can decide to perform an action that your partner may have been asking you to perform for a long time, such as taking out the trash. When you take the initiative and carry out the action even before your partner tries to suggest the action to you, you will show your partner that you respect their opinions and that you actually listened when they made complaints about that particular action of yours.

No relationship consists of just one person, and thus, you have to put that into consideration whenever you are making plans or decisions. If you have not been pulling your weight before, this is a great opportunity for you to show care and affection to them.

### *Do not expect your partner to read your mind*

A lot of people walk around with the assumption that their partners are supposed to realize whenever they are not feeling okay, when they are sick, depressed, etc. they expect that their partner is supposed to take one look at their face, decipher the precise issue with the individual, and then seek to provide solace for the said partner. Of course, in an ideal world where individuals have telepathic abilities, all of those would be possible so couples know what is wrong with their partner at any point.

Communication is key in a relationship, so whenever you feel uncomfortable or sad, you should make sure that you explain the situation to your partner. It is possible that you may genuinely not be in the mood to talk about whatever challenges you are going through. In this case, you can simply tell your partner that you will inform them when you are comfortable. Make sure that you give them the details of what happened whenever you are comfortable enough to talk about it.

Do not make the mistake of giving your partner the silent treatment. As an adult who is in a relationship, it is expected that you should have outgrown the stage of life where you communicate your hurt feelings to your partner by giving them the silent treatment. However hurt you are, having a head-on conversation about the problem is the best way of resolving conflict. Having it linger while being passive-aggressive can cause irreparable damage to your relationship. So, promptly address any issue that may arise. As soon as you are aware of any problems, immediately bring it to the attention of your partner.

### *Pick up non-verbal cues*

An emotionally intelligent person knows that a lot goes into every conversation. Thus, to communicate effectively, you need not only to be clear and precise about whatever it is you are saying, but you also have to listen keenly in order to respond effectively to whatever it is your partner is saying to you. However, apart from that, you also have to make sure that you are observant, and in that way be able to pick up non-verbal cues from your partner beyond what they are saying to you.

So, whenever you are having a conversation with your partner, look beyond what they are saying to how they are actually saying it. The tone, attitude, and even the facial expression can be cues from which you could pick up vital pieces of information that may help you clearly interpret what your partner is saying to you. In this sort of situation, you will come to the understanding that the irritation that you think is in your partner's tone could actually just be exhaustion. A lot of times, it is only when one pays attention to non-verbal cues that they would be able to pick out the clues that would help them better appreciate their partner.

Finally, the advice given here may not work in every situation. They are not a cure-all. Some of them may not work for you, especially considering that every situation and couple are different. For instance, if your partner is averse to touch, it would be counterintuitive to want to share touch with them simply because it is given as a suggestion here. It is expected that you consider your particular situation, then look for the points raised here that can address your particular relationship arrangement and then go ahead and apply it.

The aim is that by the end of this book, communication with your partner in the relationship would have improved tremendously. It may be wise to share this book with your partner. Direct them to read this book if you are currently having issues with your communication. In fact, you may even give them the book in anticipation of the day you will encounter any challenges in your communication. Do not forget that the most crucial thing to learn in communicating with your partner is that you are in it together, so for it to work, you both have to also put in the work together.

## Chapter 6: The Benefits of Good Communication

It is possible to express emotions and personal needs to one's partner in a way that is understandable for the partner both verbally and non-verbally. It is also possible to understand the needs and emotions of the partner by listening to them and observing lucidly, without prejudice that hinders the acceptance of the other. In every relationship, good communication is vital and healthy for the growth and survival of the relationship. It is understandable that every relationship has its ups and downs, but these clichés that come with being in a relationship are avoided by being able to clearly express how you feel and the things you want and how you want all this satisfied to your partner. Good communication helps your relationship to be stronger and healthier as you and your partner discuss vital situations in the relationship. Often, people talk to us about good communication in a relationship and how it is vital that we learn how to express our emotions to our partner to strengthen the relationship, but few go out of their way to properly explain what 'good communication' entails in this context and how couples can achieve it collectively.

Communication in its simplest form is the transfer of information from one place to the other. As already stated, communication is vital, but 'good communication' is indispensable. Good communication entails sharing one's view and emotions in such a manner that the addressee does not doubt and is not confused about the message the addresser intends to pass down. Learning how to communicate well with your partner is highly necessary. One might find oneself on an aimless voyage of wants and needs, anger, bitterness, and the like because we feel no one understands or can empathize with us, whereas the problem is with us the addresser who has failed to master the trick of good communication in a relationship.

Good communication entails clear communication. It is important to learn how to talk in a relationship. No matter how much you understand and love your partner, you cannot read your partner's mind, and as such, it is important that you speak up and express what is on your mind to your partner to clear up confusion and any other negative emotions that may spring up from lack of clear expression. Failure to communicate what we feel or need may lead the other partner to hate, anger, resentment, or confusion. This is because failure to express how we feel leaves the other partner at surface level. You might not know that your partner perceives that you are trying to keep a secret when what is on your mind is actually that you love your partner lots and would like to surprise them and as such don't want to let the cat out of the bag. But, if you are not strategic at expressing your emotions and at the same time, keeping the surprise away from your partner, you might leave the other partner hurt and feel neglected. All the feelings discussed above could arise in this situation because one partner has misunderstood the other. All of this wouldn't happen if partners learn to clearly express themselves to each other. People in a relationship have different communication needs and styles and must therefore strive to understand the patterns of the other partner. Whatever style you choose to communicate with your partner, ensure it is worth the time and effort. It is important to understand the other person to be able to clearly communicate with them. Some partners are shy, some are chatterboxes, others are reserved, and so on. It is important to put all this into consideration when communicating with a partner. When you talk to your partner, try to take out the time to listen to them without distractions from other people, your phone, laptop, or any other gadget.

Women are psychologically more emotional in a relationship and are tilted towards craving for attention most times. When talking to a female partner, you must give her the attention she needs. She is sharing her thoughts with you because she wants to be listened to and told that everything is alright if it's a problem she is facing. It works the other way around too. A man psychologically expects respect from one he calls his partner more than from any other person. The ego (whether subtle or blatant) could set in when it comes to the relationship. It is left to the woman to master how to disclose her thoughts and needs or complaints, whatever may be the case in a manner that does not shrink the respect you have for your male partner. You should take out time to think when communicated to. I will refer back to the example of the partner who wishes to keep a surprise from being spilled to the partner but ends up looking like they were keeping a secret from them. You are not in a competition that grades you on how fast you can think or come up with a reasonable answer. You are in a relationship as half of a whole. Understanding this would help you be at peace in communicating with your partner and do it well. Think of your thoughts on what has been said by your partner and also try to understand the angle your partner is coming from. There is a way you can communicate with your partner about your demeanor without spilling the surprise of whatever you have for them, which you do not want them to know at that particular time.

Make your statement/expression clear so that it is accurate to your partner and so they also understand it. We talked about clear communication and understanding the kind of person that your partner is to be able to know how to communicate to them. To aid you in clear communication, use the word 'I' to take responsibility for your expectations and thoughts and how you feel. 'I need' and 'I want' are expressions that could aid your communication. How do you feel? Would you prefer it if your partner did not constantly pat your back in public because it makes you feel small? Do you hate it when your partner talks a lot in public or spills too much of the secrets between you? Say it in a manner where your partner understands exactly what you are saying and how you feel about it. For example, it is one thing to tell your partner that you do not like them patting you in public and it is another thing to tell your partner that patting you on the back makes you feel small and dependent. You have to explain things to your partner in the context of how you feel. How does being patted on the back in public make you feel small? Is your partner taller than you are? Is that why you feel small in public? Understand how you feel and why you feel the way you feel. Would you feel small if your partner had patted you on the back in the privacy of your bedroom and not in public? If this question is answered in the negative then perhaps you are battling with issues of pride in your relationship. You should be open enough to tell your partner this. If this were the case, tell your partner that you feel small if patted in public but do not feel the same if it is done in the privacy of your bedroom. If you feel that what you want your partner to do in public is to hug or kiss you in public instead of patting you, then you tell them openly. It is imperative that you build your relationship on the foundation of openness so as to accommodate each other. This way, your partner can freely tell you about a person who made passes at them at work or on their way back home without knowing that they were in a relationship, and you both can laugh about it. If one of you is jealous, the other partner may notice the change in attitude of the other partner so you both should be willing to talk about it. Another secret of good communication in a relationship is talking about issues when they come up. If you do not like the fact that your partner drives a pretty colleague home every day from work and sometimes picks her up when she could comfortably find her way then you should not hide it. Take it up the moment you notice it and get it done with. Remember to be as open as possible. If you don't, you are building up resentment and hate and any negative feeling you can think of, and there is no telling what these feelings can lead you to do once it's been suppressed for too long and you suddenly explode.

When addressing how you feel to your partner, mind the tone of your voice. Don't sound demanding, authoritative, or demeaning. Negotiate and remember that you do not have to be right all the time. Learn to compromise, or put more subtly, learn to agree to disagree. Be willing to say something positive about your partner and be readily willing to say something you admire about your partner. This is particularly necessarily especially when you are pointing out negative characteristics of your partner which you do not like. It is usually a good idea to not completely make your partner feel worthless and totally negative in their character or attitude, so remind them of something unique about them. Be natural about this.

Where your verbal communication fails, your non-verbal communication could strive, or you could have the two work together. When you talk, the tone of your voice, your posture, and the expression on your face say a lot more than the words that come out of your mouth. Imagine saying 'I love you' with a flat, bored, nonchalant tone. It sends the wrong signal and does not match up with what you have said. You need an emotion strong enough to match the words coming from your mouth. Alternatively, you could use your body language to communicate how you feel to your partner. The same rule that concerns good communication also applies here. You should be ready to convey your message in words if your partner does not understand your non-verbal communication. The idea of openness also comes in here, because you would have to be very open with your partner to help them notice certain things you want them to in your body language, even when you have not said a word to them yet. You might want to take some time to calm down before communicating with your partner if you are angry.

It is important that you learn good listening skills in your relationship. Learning to listen with your full attention in your relationship helps you when it is your turn to talk to your partner. It helps you communicate well. In listening to your partner, maintain comfortable eye contact. Maintaining eye contact with someone would be dependent on culture. If it's a relationship between yourself and your parents, then your culture might not allow you look straight into your parent's eyes while speaking with them, but that is irrelevant in this discourse because this is centered on a relationship. Lean towards your partner when listening to them and show concern and interest. Do not let your partner feel like they are bored with you; it discourages good communication from your partner. Be empathetic in the manner you speak to your partner. Sit facing your partner and not sideways to them. Sit also in such a manner that you don't have to constantly look up or down just to get what your partner is saying. Your posture would help to encourage your partner to speak freely to you. Before listening to your partner, maintain a nonjudgmental mind and be ready to listen to your partner without any preconceived prejudices. Even if there are any, you should do more to ensure that your partner does not see this. It would be a bad situation to have them feeling like what they plan on saying is irrelevant because you have made up your mind about what it is all about or why they feel that way. Try not to engage in distracting activities while listening to your partner. Fidgeting with a pen, phone, book or anything, or tapping your feet on the ground constantly or acting in a hurry might dissuade the other person from fully expressing themselves because they already feel like they are a burden and would not want to keep feeling that way. Don't interrupt your partner except if it is extremely necessary and important that you say what you wish to say at that point. Cutting your partner short might cut the flow of their communication.

Some things are difficult to communicate, not because they are abstract or are insignificant to the situations of the partners but because discussing such things makes the person feel pain, anger, vulnerable, etc. It is important to learn how to control your emotions and perhaps be on top of your feelings rather than letting your emotions take over. In situations like this, if you are unable to communicate with your partner, then you both could see a counselor. Most relationship counselors are usually trained to understand the patterns in communication and to find ways to remedy them.

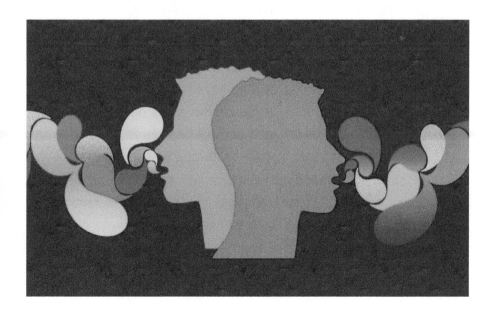

## Chapter 7: The Importance of Sex for Couples

Try asking yourself this question: would most people who eat cake do so without icing on top? Obviously not. This does not mean that one cannot eat the cake without icing, but the latter is necessary to enjoy the flavor of the cake. The icing here is what sex is in a relationship. While a relationship does not cease to be a relationship simply because the couples are not having sex, sex is a necessity in a marriage. It is an act that aids in enjoying the flavor of a relationship. The benefits of sex for a couple differ in the way people view it. Various studies have continued to show us the unlimited benefits of sexual intimacy in a relationship and outside a relationship. In marriage, the most notable benefit is the reduction in divorce rate amongst couples. While there is no fixed sexual frequency that would make it definite that divorce would not come up in a marriage and neither is it definite that continuous sex in a marriage would prevent divorce, sex remains an accessory and is necessary in a marriage.

Psychologically, sex has its effects on the mind which increases the overall well-being of the body. Studies have shown that sex helps keep couples happy and quality sex helps keep couples happier. Sex is not mandatory, so it's not something that must be fixed to be done at any particular time. The reason for this is that one partner or both of you might not be in the mood to have sex and if the reason why you arranged sex at a specific time is to get closer to each other and further strengthen your relationship, then compulsory sex might bring you both apart instead of together. Learn to have sex with your partner naturally, discuss ways to increase your sexual intimacy. Quality sex helps to relieve you of stress. Chronic stress is a given in every relationship, especially where children are concerned or a time-consuming career. Medical research has proven that the human body secretes calories and adrenaline, which respond to stress. In responding to stress, these hormones increase fatigue and high blood pressure. Increased sex is a good stress management technique. As couples grow older, they tend to grow tired and busier and become less interested in sex. However, increased sex as couples grow older helps relieve a lot of stress associated with growing old in the relationship. Sex releases some other hormones, which helps improve couple's mood in a relationship. For example, endorphins help reduce feelings of depression and loneliness. Touching the nipples releases oxytocin, which could help increase feelings of contentedness and satisfaction, and the release of prolactin when couples reach orgasm helps the body relax and induces sleep. The feeling of relaxation which sex gives can last even until the next day. Constant sex helps boost your self-esteem and increases trust in each other.

Intuitively, sex improves emotional health, but it's physical benefits are of great importance to couples. Constant sex helps to improve physical fitness, and the activities involved are most times likened to an actual exercise. The American Health Association has said that the activities involved in sexual intimacy are equivalent to walking briskly or running up a flight of 2 stairs or jogging around the block. This sexual activity holds the same advantage that constant exercise holds for the body. As already discussed, the hormone released at orgasm helps relax the nerves and induces sleep. This could help prevent stored up stress and lower the possibility of reacting negatively to stress. The calories released within the 30 - 40 minutes of sexual intimacy helps reduce fat and makes the body fitter. Certain chemicals are released during sex that also help reduce cravings. Sexual intimacy helps improve the workings of the immune system; this is because the heat shared during intimacy helps prevent flu and cold. The cardiac effects of sex also abound. Sex helps to lower blood pressure. Increased blood pressure can put a strain on the cardiac vessels causing a stroke or other severe heart disease. When sexual intimacy is engaged in by couples, it slows down activities of vessels and allows increased flow of nutrients and oxygen to places where it is largely needed to protect the heart. It is important to include that sex can precipitate a heart attack where there is risk. The reason for this is that sex is like every other exercise which involves straining the muscles, engaging in strenuous activity, and the possibility of the respiratory rate increasing and blood pressure increase is likely, which eventually would lead to cardiac diseases. Studies have proven that more sex helps increase the brains cognition and helps in the production of new brain cells. Other health benefits of sex would include glowing skin as a result of the continuous release of DHEA during sexual intimacy, and faster digestion, healthier teeth, and increased sense of smell are all medical findings that have come far to support the importance of sex. Sex helps increase a man's sexual libido, and it helps lubricate the woman's vaginal region. Also, reduction in sexual cramps has most times been attached to sexual intimacy.

In a relationship, constant sexual intimacy helps increase the couple's commitment to one another and also help them connect emotionally.

## Chapter 8: The Importance of Having Fun to Couples

A strong, healthy, happy, and long-lasting relationship does not just happen. It is a conscious effort by both parties, where each partner sees to the betterment of the relationship and each other in all ramifications. Dull, droll, lazy, boring, and annoying are definitely what you'd want your relationship to be described as. Fun-filled, interesting, happy, and joyful are better words you would want your relationship to be described with. It is understandable that things change in a relationship, and things move from how they were at the very beginning where you both met to become more mundane. With increased meetings, house chores, jobs, children, and other impromptu activities that spring up here and there in a relationship, it is only important that couples find a way to balance every part of their lives. The importance of being spontaneous and playful in your relationship cannot be overemphasized. It takes away the burden of having to constantly sit down and speak you mind and painstakingly explain certain things to your partner because when having downtime, there is a bond that is fostered. Your partner knows you more and can figure out your boundaries. Having fun with each other in a relationship helps increase your affection for each other. Imagine saying something and having the other person laugh so hard and then noticing that they have a particular trait about them you never noticed. The relationship is strengthened when you are reminded that the source of the other person's laughter and joy is you. The implication of this is that the possibility of you both getting a divorce anytime soon is very low if at all existent. Couples who have fun are happy and tend to spread this happiness around even beyond their relationship. It rubs off on the kids, in the church, at the office, and even amongst the people in the neighborhood. While it might be easy to fake that you have it all rosy at home, or that you dread going home every time it is mentioned, having to pretend is not healthy.

In a relationship, there is nothing more important than being united. Your ability to stand for your partner, come what may, is often as a result of coming to know them through constantly interacting and having fun with them. Having fun with your partner breeds unity; you learn to forgive quickly, you learn to overlook certain acts of the other person even before they apologize. It does not mean you should allow your partner to take you for granted or be manipulative. Ensure that being playful with your partner does not rob you both of communication and the other necessary factors for a healthy relationship. If your partner is one who constantly gets you angry without seeing the need to apologize (or if their apology never sounds like they are sorry), then you might want to sit and work that out before allowing it to slide and perhaps breed more negativity in your relationship. Don't allow constant fun between yourself and your partner take the place of real apology in your relationship when your partner has done something wrong. An apology is appropriate, and it could be done playfully so long as they mean their apology, and you do not feel shortchanged in your relationship. Another benefit of being playful with your partner is that it breeds hope. Hope for better things to come in the future. It is not unusual to see people in marriages as if they cannot wait for it to end (even after saying 'till death do us part'). It should not be that way. Many times, the reason for this feeling is that couples have lost hope in the marriage - they feel they are merely passengers in the marriage instead of the drivers of their marriage who take charge. What hope does for you is that it assures you of the future even when you do not know what that future holds for you two. Having fun with your partner reassures you and keeps you optimistic about the relationship. There's just that joy when you rough and tumble, and laugh with your partner, that assures you everything will be alright between you guys. This is what hope is all about; you are positive in fun times with your partner that the future will be better and that whatever hurdles are present can be overcome. Being playful in your marriage rubs off on your children as they grow and your children are the best legacy you can leave the world with. No one wants to have annoying, angry, and sad children around them. Statistics have shown that nurturing kids in a happy environment tends to boost their positive outlook and helps them strive for better things in life. Children who grow up in a happy and playful environment tend to be more optimistic, and they approach failure as a stepping stone rather than a setback. Your playfulness as a couple also rubs off on your family at times. There are stories of marriages that have survived the hostility of family members (perhaps because the couples are from different countries or religions and the family members did not support the marriage) simply by being constantly happy in their marriage.

What then does it mean for couples to enjoy some recreation time in their relationship? Having fun with your partner could be described as a pleasurable manner of having fun at a discretionary time. Of course, our definitions of what is pleasurable in a relationship may differ. But, taking from the analogy of cake, fun time with your partner is the icing which should not be sacrificed. Research has shown that having fun and bonding in a relationship is not only a pleasurable activity but also a form of developmental activity. Just like the way children, while growing, learn a lot from interacting with their peers and playing games and having conversations, we also learn a lot about our partner from playing with them. It was Plato, a Greek philosopher, who said that what could you learn about a person in one hour of laughing and having fun with them, might not be even be understood about that person in one year of conversation. So, in having fun with your partner, you learn a lot about them and yourself. For example, how your partner reacts to losing a game played with you might just be the way they would react when they are let go from a job or lose someone dear to them. The manner your partner behaves during certain moments might just be indicative of what they would do in the real world. It will show if they are the type that takes responsibility for their actions, if they laugh at and look down on others who have experienced failure with pride, or if they treat people like they are part of the same team. Recreation time with a partner reveals to you a lot about your partner, and this knowledge can be garnered covertly, as opposed to typical dialogues.

Some persons see recreation time as childish. There is a video on the internet of a groom who had slapped the bride on their wedding day, simply because she had tried to be playfully mischievous with their wedding cake as she attempted to feed him. The point is, playful activities in relationships are not taboo. We should not be ashamed of them. You probably shouldn't say things like this to your partner: "lower your voice and stop laughing like a kid, the neighbors will hear us." While every relationship does not function in the same way, how about loosening up a bit? Nothing positive, good, or healthy comes out of a relationship unless the partners have consciously worked towards making it happen. An interesting fact here is that many people, before agreeing to be in a relationship with someone, may not mind the fun and games. There is a possibility that this all changes upon entering a relationship. By this time, it becomes immature to laugh in a certain way or behave in a playful manner. It's quite funny when people see or interpret playfulness in relationships as an act of childishness. The advantages of being happy in a relationship are not debatable, and neither are the advantages of being playful. It's important to state here that being playful in a relationship does not guarantee everything that has been explained above in the form of advantages, but the possibilities of these advantages coming forth are quite high. Here are some tips you should consider to spice up your relationship.

### Schedule time for fun

Most couples intend to have fun but never really get around their business schedule or household chores or dealing with kids to really have fun. Fix a time for recreation on the calendar. If some time is allotted for you both to have fun, then you would get around having done so one way or the other.

### Spontaneity

You should not make having fun bureaucratic or mandatory. Make your relationship as spontaneous as is reasonable considering what both of you are used to and can adjust to. Having fun should not be a do or die affair, it should be something that you do because you want to enjoy each other's company and not because the calendar says so. It's important that you find time for downtime at some point in your relationship. The reason why a calendar is important is for situations when you have been so busy for too long that (though you are not quarreling or drifting apart from your partner) you no longer have time to throw funny jabs at each other.

### Variety

As already discussed, have fun should be pleasurable and could and should include playing games, going to the movies together, having sex, looking at old pictures together, etc., so long as it involves something pleasurable that keeps you both happy and promotes intimacy. To help you and your partner spend more time having fun, it is important you learn healthy habits and try to exude positive energy all the time.

### Willingness and Health Consciousness

Most times, when couples have agreed to recreation time, or when one partner feels like having a little fun, they might end up not doing so with each other because one person is either too lazy or unwilling to. Even when we find the space in our busy schedules to spend some quality time together, we may find ourselves drained for some reason. It is therefore important that both partners encourage each other to eat healthily and exercise more often. Eat together as a couple, and if your partner is exercising, join them. If you both encourage each other to exercise, then you could utilize this as an opportunity to bond and have fun together.

### Loosen Up

Give yourself the opportunity to be a kid once in a while in your relationship. Be open to new things, and don't let your relationship make you lose your wonder. Look forward to new things and be ever ready to learn, especially when it has to do with new and untried ways of having fun with your partner. Be willing to speak to your partner about anything. Communicate your fears and concerns about things to them. This is wisdom about communication that can be learned from little kids. Most times, we get so caught up in being perfect adults that we forget how to be kids or begin to see being playful as being childish. It's not childish to tickle your partner out of the blue when tickling them makes them laugh. Learn to confide in your partner. It's easier to find the voice to tell your partner uncomfortable things when you both are out having a good old playtime.

### Compromise

In your relationship, it's important to be spontaneous and learn to be open to new things. Your idea of fun and games might not be the same as that of your partner, but this is where compromise, sacrifice, and dialogue come into play. If your partner asks that you both try something new, then be open to it. It might be something you are not used to or have never done before, but variety is the spice of life. You should make trying new things the spice of your relationship. It is not recommended that you do something that is negative or that you are averse to. Remember that the idea is to do new things that would boost your affection for your partner and help your relationship and yourself better, so if this new activity would not do this for you then you should not engage in it. Try to protect your fun time from conflicts and resentment. It is important, as was discussed earlier, that you clear all grievances which you and your partner may have against each other before having fun.

### Forgiveness

You might, understandably, have reservations about entertaining games, jokes, and other playful activities with your partner if you are still harboring some sort of resentment against them. But if you allow yourself to have some fun with them, you might find yourself understanding and forgiving them. Still, this depends on the level of the grievance, as some things may hurt too much to let go of easily.

Then, you must decide if you want the relationship to work. It might be impossible to actually have fun with someone while harboring resentment towards them. Let your mind be free and in the moment. You shouldn't let any pent-up anger prevent you from having fun with your partner if you both are still interested in making the relationship work.

### Budgeting

One other thing to discuss with your partner, as it concerns recreation time, is budgeting. It might seem trivial that you have to save money just to have fun with your partner, especially when you have other pressing needs to deal with. But it may be useful to set some money aside to grow the affection and love in your relationship because this is what having fun actually does for your relationship. It's possible to find activities that are not very expensive or that do not cost a dime. Just ensure that when it comes to having fun, you do not let the absence of funds limit yourself and your partner from doing so.

### Team Spirit

Learn to have fun as a team. This is especially important if you are the type that is excessively competitive. You might begin to see having fun, when playing games, swimming together, and so on, as an avenue to win and prove to the other person how much better you are at that particular activity than they are. Unhealthy competition amongst couples do not strengthen a relationship, it tears them apart. Learning to have fun and not be concerned about winning or losing to your partner is important. After all, you guys, as partners, are members of the same team. You must train your mind to think in this way. Engage in activities in which you cannot play or have fun without the other person's active participation.

### Write it Down

If you are the type that takes having fun and playing with your partner very seriously (you should be), then it would be okay to sit with your partner once in a while to discuss what you both believe is limiting your fun time. How can you both make it better? What does the other person enjoy doing? It would be effective if you both write out what your ideas of fun are separately and then come together and go through them to determine what should be considered and what should be discarded. Note that you should not make this a mechanical process. Be honest and playful even as you write about the fun things you would like to do with your partner. But, do not forget that the purpose of doing this is so that you and your partner can understand each other's boundaries and what you both are willing to give a try. While you may want to start encouraging your partner to enjoy certain activities they have expressed no interest in, you should be careful in the manner you go about this. It does not mean that you both cannot subsequently try out new things outside what you have drafted, so long as it is related to what you guys consider fun and are both comfortable with them. The idea is to keep the fun alive.

### Couple's Retreat

If all else fails, then you could both go for a couple's retreat. This is usually a fun time scheduled with a relationship coach or therapist.

These people are trained to understand the nuances of relationships and the psychology of people and are able to connect the dots. Many of which you and your partner might not easily notice. Conversing as a couple and trying to have fun in the presence of a coach will encourage bonding with the help of a person trained to help your relationship grow stronger.

## Chapter 9: Sexual Intimacy in a Relationship: How to Improve It with Communication?

You and your partner are different individuals with different hormones and chemistry, leading you both to act separately. You may not be sexually excited by the same things as your partner, or may do so at different times. You may be in the mood, but they are not or vice versa. You try to make a move, but they shove you off. You feel bitter and embarrassed because this is someone you love, and when people who we love hurt us, we feel the pain on a higher scale than when it is done by other regular people. Now, you've decided to stay away from your partner and may start talking about how you will get back at them — how you will also turn down their sexual advances when they are in the mood. You want to pay them back in their own coin. You are upset, and your partner is frustrated at your behavior because they really are not interested in having sex at that moment. They feel themselves caught between trying to satisfy you (against their comfort) and sticking to their guns. Now, the both of you are mad at each other's behavior. You begin to wonder why you and your partner cannot just have good sex and intimate sexual moments. You have tried various supplements and herbs to boost you and your partner's libido, but they don't work as advertised. You both are barely ever sexually intimate. You are frustrated because all around you are people who have great sex without batting an eyelid and yet you cannot. You ask: Shouldn't sex be better in marriage? Shouldn't it be more interesting, with both parties willing to partake? But the reverse is the case in your situation. You barely get enough sex in your marriage, and you want more.

The solutions to such situations are not mysterious. You have all it takes to make your partner get back on track with being sexually intimate with you. But, remember that there is no hard and fast rule about it.

When your partner loses interest in having sex with you, it might not necessarily mean that they are no longer in love with you (although, there are some cases where the absence of love is the reason). A partner who loses interest in having sex with you might just be bored with the continuous monotone in your sex life - it could be a bad habit in your sex life that you have refused to stop that could be turning them off, it could be that you have constantly turned your partner off too many times that they have now become used to not having any sexual feelings for you. We could paint many more instances and still have a lot more on the list. But, when a partner does not express sexual desire for their partner, one must not conclude that they are into someone else or that they have fallen out of love.

Why do people get into relationships? The answer to this question should be quite simple: people want to be intimate (sexually, emotionally, intellectually, etc.) with another person. They want to be able to rely on someone and share their soul with that individual. As human beings, we yearn for another's touch, love, attention, and closeness. We want to be able to speak freely with someone and feel a sense of belonging. It is, therefore, normal to get all angry and hurt when we get rejected when it comes to sexual intimacy by someone we love so much. It would seem that the idea of intimacy has been largely reduced only to sex. Intimacy involves being physically close to a person. You could be physically close to someone in a manner that does not entail having sex. The point, however, is that sex is a very important necessity in a marriage, and as such, every issue of sexual intimacy links back to the topic of sex. Being sexually intimate could include kissing, cuddling, taking a shower together, hugging, sex, and the list goes on. Other forms of intimacy that are not physical are emotional and intellectual intimacy, heart-to-heart conversations, and spiritual intimacy. True marital intimacy comes with being honest with your partner and being vulnerable with your partner. This may be difficult, but it shows that you have come to trust and lean on your partner so much that you believe they have your best interests at heart and will not hurt you. It means that you are willing to go through the risks of what may come out of your genuine trust for your partner. Being vulnerable in a relationship does not connote weakness. Put more appropriately, it means that you have taken charge of your life enough in the relationship to be able to trust your partner with it. You should not expect what you do not have to give. As such, to trust in someone so much in a relationship that we expect honesty from them means that, first and foremost, you are honest with yourself.

When it comes to emotional intimacy, couples should be willing to share their joy, laughter, fear, sorrow, frustration, depression, and even anger. You should be free to bring up how you feel to your partner properly without fear. Sharing what has you angry, is not an excuse for you to hurt your partner with scathing words. Don't allow yourself to get so upset that you hit them, or even try to. In sharing your anger, you should be willing to sit your partner down and tell them what they have done that you do not like which has gotten you irritated and angry. It means that you should be able to take charge of your relationship and be responsible for what happens in the relationship. Understand that in a relationship you are half of a couple and not the whole, you both need each other to make it work so you both must be willing to share your anger, sorrow, depression, and frustrations as much as you are willing to share your laughter and joy. Couples must be as free as a bird with each other, and while it is advised to control your anger and not lash out, it is also advisable that you do not bottle up your feelings. If it makes you feel better to yell when you are angry, then, by all means, suit yourself. But make sure that your partner is not inconvenienced by the same action that puts you at ease. Also, even if you are angry, there is no reason to also be condescending. Put simply, correct each other with love. Emotional intimacy is one of the strongest bonds in a couple, and it can break if couples share emotional conversations had with their partner with their co-worker, online, parents, etc. It is important to consider your partner's emotional status in seeking help. You might be willing to seek advice from any of your parents or in-laws, but your partner might not be and they might take this as a betrayal of the trust they have put in you. It is advisable that you run many of the actions you are about to take by your partner, instead of selfishly expecting them to go along with decisions you came to by yourself. To not involve your partner in this way could imply that you have no respect for them.

Intellectual intimacy involves engaging both of your minds in any topic. It could be seeing a movie and discussing the scenes or reading a book together and sharing your views on the plot of the book or the ideas canvassed in the book. What is your take on certain societal or economic issues, and what is your partner's take on them? Intellectual intimacy has nothing to do with educational equivalence. It has nothing to do with what you studied or what school you attended different from that which your spouse attended. Intellectual intimacy connotes finding something that needs both you and your spouse's yearning to learn from each other. It is usually tempting when sharing emotional intimacy to want to make remarks that discredit the other person's knowledge or school while boasting one's own knowledge and institutions of learning. Couples should be careful when sharing their knowledge on issues to be as neutral as possible in dealing with their partners. It is usually advisable to give our views on a particularly controversial matter without having to juxtapose one's view with that of the partner to point out how the partner's views are flawed and unintelligent. If at all you point out why you have made your argument and the reasons why your partner's arguments are not the best solution to the problem then you must do so in a manner that is welcoming and loving. Or better still, you could correct the manner that you would want yourself to be corrected if you were in their position. Heart-to-heart conversations are just conversations that help to develop sexual, intellectual, and emotional intimacy. It does not have to be premised on a particular topic. Just you and your partner reconnecting with each other. It could be you sharing a silly joke about something that happened between yourself and your partner some time ago or a funny event that occurred while you were still in school. It does not have to be anything momentous. What name would we give our child? What is your next move regarding your job? It goes on and on.

Sometimes, conversing with your partner without words can be the best form of emotional intimacy. It does not have to be something which you both schedule to do every day. In fact, it is not. It could be looking at something at the same time with your partner and nodding at each other in understanding because it reminds you of something worth smiling about. There is a connection there between you and your partner, and it has nothing to do with words. It could be glancing at each other momentarily and just being grateful that you have each other, or mowing the lawn together, walking together, a long embracing hug when something tragic occurs in the family, etc. These activities are ways you can be deeply intimate with your partner without using words. Being intimate with your partner is something that is built on years of staying together, fighting together, laughing together, crying together, and so on. It takes having lived through the good and bad times with a person to be able to share something significant with them even without communicating with words. It involves trust and honesty, and as was stated earlier, compromising in your relationship. Remember that, in a relationship, you shouldn't hold back. You should trust your partner enough to share your secrets, ideas, and worries freely with them. The absence of this may result in your relationship not lasting very long.

Spiritual intimacy is not a cliché. A family that prays together stays together. It is not unusual to find people who attach the greatest importance to their marriage. It is okay to accept vulnerability and take your concerns to a trusted and close family member if you cannot solve them. But it cannot be overstressed that you share this decision with your partner before going ahead with it. Some people prefer to not discuss their relationship issues with a third party, unless they are convinced otherwise. It is important that you do not look for quick fixes to your relationship, such as believing that God would solve your issues with no effort from you. There is, practically, no hope for a lasting relationship or enjoying the deep and meaningful sexual intimacy in a relationship if we do not work for it. How then should a couple go about achieving intimacy in their marriage?

Encourage physical intimacy in your marriage. Snuggle, kiss, hold hands, and talk to each other, sleep close to each other naked without necessarily having sex. It's a way to physically connect with your partner. Learn to bathe together as a couple. Washing each other and giving massages in the bath grows your physical and emotional intimacy. It helps couples get closer to each other and have sex more often. Remember that there are no hard and fast rules about having the best relationship. Treat each other the way you both did when you first started dating. Look for those little acts that tickled your partner's fancy while you both were still dating and try applying it again. It is quite simple to do the things your partner loves. Learn to communicate with each other on a deeper level. Learn to share your struggles, dreams, and passions with your partner. Let your partner know about things going on in your life which they may not see by merely looking at you. This way, you both eliminate keeping secrets from each other and also connect more emotionally and sexually. Leave love notes for your partner around the house. Surprise them with a lunch box at work. Buy them flowers and decorate the house with it in your partner's name. Leaving love notes in your partner's purse, laptop case, suit pocket, or on the table in the bedroom could help your partner feel loved, cherished, and remembered. Your partner wants to believe that even though you are not physically together, you have them in kind all the time. They want to be reassured that they are on your mind, and this is the impression you give them when you perform thoughtful gestures.

Experiment with sex using different positions and styles. Use lubricants to bring pleasure to each other. If you both are going to try out a new style or position which neither of you know anything about, you could go online and do some research. There is some research to suggest that pornography could be used to boost sexual creativity in relationships. If you must employ this method, then ensure that it is for the purpose of helping both you and your partner in the sexual department of your relationship and that you both view the pornography sites together. It is not advisable that you go on a porn site alone, especially where one is alone or in a long-distance relationship, as this could lead to addiction. Ensure that you both are looking out for each other in your quest to become sexually intimate. If all other actions fail, then you both can see a specialist. No relationship is perfect. There are going to be times when the whole ordeal of love and staying together forever could seem blurry and no longer achievable. In situations like this, we must reach into our hearts for the love we still feel for then, remembering whatever it is that drew you to your partner in the first place and then make it work for the sake of you and your partner. This, in itself, is the purest act of intimacy.

## Chapter 10: How Communication Helps You Deal with Relatives and Friends: For Married and Unmarried Couples Who Live Together

There is the story of a woman who married at the age of 22. Before her marriage, she had very close friends with whom she always hung around with and was always seen with. She was her parents' only child, and no one batted an eyelid whenever she asked for anything. The couple's house was given to her by her parents. Her husband was well to do and very wealthy, and he was comfortable with the marriage and his wife. What he was not comfortable with was the fact that the friends and parents of his wife failed to understand that the woman and himself were now married and that it was not necessary for her mom to call her every night to be sure 'her husband fed her', to be sure she had fun, and to tell them if she had any issues or disagreements with her husband that day. Also, her friends visited constantly (without first calling to ask if they could come around). The husband soon became frustrated in his own house and marriage. This brings us to the question: how do you separate your new married life from your former single life. How do you go about it without hurting anyone?

It is important, first, to recognize that that once you get married to your partner, you are now a unit. A unit in the sense that you are now the primary support for each other. In a healthy marriage, you would most likely turn to your partner for help before going to anyone else. For married couples, you become independent of your parents and siblings, no matter how reliant you were on them before your marriage. This is something else to discuss with your partner, to ensure you both see the relationship in the same way. Marriage is an entirely different ball game from the life you lived as a single woman or man. Be ready for responsibilities and be willing to take them as they come. We all have our pasts, and for this reason, you must begin to realize how to not let your former single life interfere with your present relationship. You must start setting some rules for yourself, such as sharing your whereabouts with your partner and being time conscious so as not to have them worry. This is even more true if you both live together. But understand that you are not expected to become a monk when you enter a relationship. You should live your life as you want to, as you still need some amount of space and freedom to make your relationship work. The help of experienced people in a relationship, like your parents and others, may be needed in your relationship.

If you are living with your partner, you should subtly tell your friends or parents to inform you before coming around. If your friends come around without first telling you, explain that you were not aware of their visit to your partner. Especially if your partner is uncomfortable with it, you must make it clear to them that sudden visits are not welcome. That way, they would be less likely to repeat the action. This is not to say you should make enemies of everyone you had been close to before the relationship. But, living with your partner implies a certain level of commitment, and you both should be allowed to explore the relationship to ascertain that you would take it further. Try to create balance in your life. You don't want to get married and have friends suddenly visit you or drop in on you without informing you.

For married couples, you should instill the reality in everyone outside the relationship that you are a married man/woman and that being married requires some rules for the new marriage to work out. Also, while working on separating your single life from your marriage life, work with your partner. No one wants to live with a partner who turns their nose up at you or a relative if the latter visits without notice. You and your partner should be on the same page as to what is acceptable and what is not with friends and relatives. If such a thing happened, do not expect your partner to pretend to enjoy their visit. You could inform your partner to subtly tell their relative to inform you both before coming over the next time. Your partner would be in a better position to relay this message because the person is their relative, and they should be closer to them than you are.

Learn to subtly communicate with your parents about your new family. If your parents give you a gift which is meant to be for your marriage, then you should seek the consent of your partner before receiving such a gift. It does not mean that you become restricted from receiving gifts from your family members when you become married, but you must understand that certain gifts should not be welcomed because of the impression they give to your marriage and the image it creates between yourself and your spouse. For example, your partner might not want you to receive gifts from other people which could give the impression that you are not getting enough from your marriage. Or in the scenario where your parents constantly shower you with gifts that are to be used by you with the exclusion of your partner. This could create the impression in the mind of your partner that you are expected to be their superior in the relationship. To avoid the rift this kind of situation may result in, you should seek your partner's consent before receiving such gifts. Remember that you are now half of a whole unit and are no longer single. You should avoid associations with people who were once your crush or with whom you had previously been in a relationship. Where there is a problem in your marriage, your first point of call may be to rekindle relationships with these people. It is natural to look for the next soul to show us care, love, and affection when your partner only ever seems to quarrel with and reject you. It is more natural for female partners to seek means of expressing their emotions and concerns to the first listening ear. Your best friend should be your husband/wife. It is important that you both learn how to look forward to being around each other, tell each other how your day went and how to solve your concerns. Sharing your problems with your partner strengthens you against going to the next willing hands at the first hint of a problem.

Learn to live with a new person, attitude, and life. Activities such as bathing alone, sleeping in a bed alone, and such other simpler things might need to be revisited and changed. Living in an understanding marriage is key. It is important that you have married someone acceptable to you in all ramifications. One that does not demand you living a pretense for the rest of your life in a bid to satisfy them. The reason why it is vital to marry someone with whom you are already free with is to enable you to both connect. It is easier in such situations to grow emotional, intellectual, and sexual intimacy and to also solve issues which ordinarily would be difficult if you both were still trying to understand each other. With everything said so far, it should not be implied that you cannot confide in your parents and friends or sisters in regard to issues in your marriage. Your in-laws could serve as a counselor in your marriage, and so can your sister or friends. What is important is to know when to draw the line. To know what to share with your family or that of your partner, you should understand that your marriage is a family made up of yourself, your partner, and your children if you have any and so you do not have to reveal a secret that is personal to your marriage.

## Chapter 11: Some Facts About Successful Relationships

In addition to all that has been shared in this book, here are some things you may or may not know about successful relationships.

### Daily recommitment

Even if your relationship is seemingly in a good place at the moment, there is no reason to stop doing all the things that got the relationship started in the first place. Through your words and actions, you should reaffirm your love and dedication to your partner. Send them romantic messages, buy them gifts, hug them for no particular reason, etc. This is necessary to keep the relationship thriving.

### Fewer arguments and more agreements

Unfortunately, there are some who have come to believe that disagreements and constant fighting in relationships are what, in a sense, make the heart grow fonder. This is not true. In fact, it is important that there are more good times than bad in the relationship. This is often stated as the hallmark of a successful relationship. Make sure the happy moments in your relationship are much more frequent than the negative ones.

### Be mindful

It is quite easy to get carried away by ambition, work, and other factors outside the relationship where we simply go through the motions with our partners. In such instances, even when you are physically in the room, your mind isn't present and you are looking forward to other things besides enjoying the moment with your partner. People can often tell when you would rather be elsewhere than with them. Do not become so familiar with your partner that the quality of your relationship deteriorates to this point. Consciously relish every second you spend with your partner.

### Be expressive

That is to say, be romantic. Not every one of us can recreate those lovey-dovey scenes from romantic movies, but this isn't necessary. Truthfully, the thought and attempt matter a lot more than anything. Simply telling your partner how much you love and care about them is good, but not enough. You must express that affection. It could be something as simple as holding their hands when you both go out for a walk.

### Don't rely on money to make it work

Sadly, the period we now live in is one that is marked by vanity. It is celebrated more now than at any other time in the past. As a consequence, the culture of winning and sacrificing for love is quickly eroding. Many are convinced that they can buy love. The reality is that any relationship built on greed has no hope of surviving. Of course, being able to afford the good things in life for your partner allows for a fun and exciting relationship, but materialism must not be the basis of your relationship.

### Don't expect perfection

Regardless of how highly you have placed your partner, understand that they are human beings like yourself. They have their beauty and flaws. They did not arrive in a box according to your specifications, and you shouldn't expect that they will, someday, become the image of perfection in your head. If you can appreciate this fact, then your relationship is set up nicely for longevity.

### Be helpful

Offer to help your partner when they need it, instead of acting like you couldn't care any less about what they are struggling with. Be ready to come to their assistance, especially when it is about something you are good with. And for the purpose of clarity, your partner needn't have to ask for your help before you give it out. You also shouldn't ask for anything in return (unless you are merely being humorous, that is). They are your teammate. Selflessness is expected of you.

## Conclusion

According to Tony Robbins, connection is number four on the list of basic needs shared by every human being. We all, regardless of our personality types, want to truly connect with at least one person. One of the best ways to do this is through communication. A lot is revealed during honest conversations and when things like trust are tended to. After all, how can you claim to connect with someone when you do not know them?

This book discussed everything from sex, the importance of having fun in a relationship, and forms of communication. The content of this book is helpful both to married and unmarried couples and is written to cater to people of varying experiences in relationships.

A lot of us understand the importance of communication in a relationship but are at a loss on how to go about it the right way. This was the purpose that the book aimed to achieve. It is my hope that you have learned, from the pages of this book, useful lessons which can be applied in your relationship. Do not merely put this book back on the shelf after reading it and continue with your life as usual. Much of the advice shared here is practical. As such, you should put them into action. This is the only way the knowledge in this book will be of any benefit to you.

If you and your partner are interested in making your relationship a success, put the wisdom shared in this book to work and watch your relationship flourish.

## References

4 types of communication styles. (2018). Retrieved July 21, 2019, from https://online.alvernia.edu/articles/4-types-communication-styles/

5 styles of communication. (2017). Retrieved July 21, 2019, from https://dspsychology.com.au/5-styles-of-communication/

Georgi. (2015). The amazing benefits of being open-minded. Retrieved July 23, 2019, from https://www.google.com/amp/s/innerouterpeace.com/benefits-of-being-open-minded/amp/

How can couples counselling benefit our relationship? (n.d.). Retrieved July 22, 2019, from https://www.couplecounselling.com.au/relationship-counselling-sydney/relationship-counselling-benefits/

Howard, L. (2017). 9 signs your partner doesn't respect you enough. Retrieved July 25, 2019, from https://www.bustle.com/p/9-signs-your-partner-doesnt-respect-you-enough-7664412

Kushnick, G. (2015). Your habit of pointing out other people's faults is ruining your life. Retrieved July 28, 2019, from https://medium.com/@DrGregKushnick/your-habit-of-pointing-out-other-people-s-faults-is-ruining-your-life-9f4483b67190

Legg, T. (2017). The effects of stress on your body. Retrieved July 25, 2019, from https://www.healthline.com/health/stress/effects-on-body#9

Powers, A. (2018). Connecting the dots: the link between innovation and open-mindedness, with insights from science. Retrieved July 24, 2019, from https://www.google.com/amp/s/www.forbes.com/sites/annapowers/2018/12/07/connecting-the-dots-the-link-between-innovation-and-open-mindedness-with-insights-from-science/amp/

Raab, D. (2017). Deep listening in personal relationships. Retrieved July 20, 2019, from https://www.google.com/amp/s/www.psychologytoday.com/us/blog/the-empowerment-diary/201708/deep-listening-in-personal-relationships%3famp

Seltzer, L. (2013). 6 signs of narcissism you may not know about. Retrieved July 25, 2019, from https://www.google.com/amp/s/www.psychologytoday.com/us/blog/evolution-the-self/201311/6-signs-narcissism-you-may-not-know-about%3famp

Steber, C. (2017). 11 surprising ways complaining can affect your health. Retrieved July 25, 2019, from https://www.bustle.com/p/11-surprising-ways-complaining-can-affect-your-health-70324

Stokes, R. (2017). 7 ways to deal with a true narcissist — before he destroys your soul. Retrieved July 28, 2019, from https://www.yourtango.com/2017307004/how-deal-narcissist-relationship

Stritof, S. (2019). How nitpicking your spouse can damage your marriage. Retrieved July 28, 2019, from https://www.verywellmind.com/dont-nit-pick-at-one-another-2302501

Stritof, S. (2019). 10 tips to become an active listener in your relationship. Retrieved July 20, 2019, from https://www.mydomaine.com/top-listening-tips-2303208

The Little Shaman. (2018). Yes, narcissists can change - here's how [Video file]. Retrieved July 28, 2019, from https://youtu.be/4Y0A4GxX5lo

CPSIA information can be obtained
at www.ICGtesting.com
Printed in the USA
BVHW061454030321
601594BV00004B/98